Inspiring Thoughts for Everyday Living

101 MOMENTS
of HOPE

EDWARD GRINNAN

Editor-in-Chief, Guideposts Magazine

Pi Pocket
INSPIRATIONS

Ellie
Claire

...inspired by life

© 2013 Ellie Claire™ Gift & Paper Corp.
a division of Worthy Media, Inc.
Brentwood, TN 37027
www.ellieclaire.com

ISBN 978-1-60936-601-8

Every attempt has been made to credit the sources of copyrighted material
used in this book. If any such acknowledgment has been inadvertently
omitted or miscredited, receipt of such information would be appreciated.

All Scripture quotations, unless otherwise noted, are taken from The King
James Version of the Bible.

Scripture quotations marked (NIV) are taken from The Holy Bible, New
International Version®, NIV®. Copyright © 1973, 1978, 1984 Biblica. Used by
permission of Zondervan. All rights reserved.

Scripture quotations marked (RSV) are taken from the Revised Standard
Version of the Bible. Copyright © 1946, 1952, 1971 by Division of Christian
Education of the National Council of Churches of Christ in the USA. Used
by permission.

Scripture quotations marked (NASB) are taken from the New American
Standard Bible®, copyright © 1960, 1962, 1963, 1968, 1971, 1972, 1973, 1975,
1977, 1995 by The Lockman Foundation. Used by permission.

Stock or custom editions of Ellie Claire titles may be purchased in bulk for
educational, business, ministry, fundraising, or sales promotional use. For
information, please e-mail info@ellieclaire.com.

Edited by Terri Castillo
Cover by Jeff and Lisa Franke
Interior design and typesetting by Jeff Jansen | aestheticsoup.net

Printed in USA.

INTRODUCTION

"I Enjoy Writing about Guacamole"

This book is a selection of the devotionals I have written for *Daily Guideposts*. But I have to tell you I never had any ambition to become a devotional writer. In fact, I did everything I could to resist it. Fortunately, Van Varner was a persistent man.

Readers of *Daily Guideposts* know Van as the former editorial director of *Guideposts* magazine and a devotional writer himself. Van had hired me as an editor, and after a few years he decided that I should be writing devotionals as well.

"I don't think I can do that, Van," I told him in his office one morning. The early sun slanting through the blinds made me squint.

Van leaned back in his chair, looking a little aggrieved. I'd declined his offer to write for *Daily Guideposts* before, but he kept bringing it up.

"Tell me why not," he said.

"I'm not that sort of person."

"No? What sort of person do you mean?"

"You know, someone who talks about himself."

Van laughed. "You talk about yourself all the time!"

"You know what I mean," I shot back.

"I'm not sure I do. You love to tell about all sorts of things...your wife, your dogs, your mom, your adventures living in New York City."

"But those aren't devotionals," I protested. "Those are just stories."

"Don't you see? Devotionals *are* stories; honest, personal stories about how we experience our lives on a daily basis from the perspective of our faith."

Maybe that was what was hanging me up—the faith part. Maybe I just didn't feel confident enough in my own spiritual life to be drawing conclusions for other people to read.

"Look," Van continued, "you came in here the other day and told a very nice story about a silly argument you and Julee had over a guacamole recipe and how in the end it brought the two of you closer. That's a devotional right there."

"You want me to write about guacamole?"

"I want you to write about yourself, Edward. That's what I mean."

Finally I relented and agreed to write the devotional about guacamole, if only to escape Van's tireless entreaties. I still thought it was an absurd undertaking. I showed it to Julee when I was done, thinking she would tell me I was nuts.

"Aw...it's sweet," she said.

Van made some suggestions and gave it back to me. I reworked it. He made more edits and said it was good. But I reworked it some more.

"What's next?" I said.

"You tell me," Van replied.

In truth, I had discovered that I actually enjoyed writing about guacamole. Recounting the fight I'd had with Julee, I was able to see our relationship in a more revealing light, a perspective I never would have gained if I hadn't written about it. Slowly but surely, as one devotional followed another, I felt my perceptions shift. I found myself seeking those spiritual lessons in daily living, and the seeking enriched my soul and deepened my faith to believe that God can touch us at any moment of our lives.

That was eighteen years and hundreds of devotionals ago. I've learned to write about practically anything, from the death of my mother to playing on the Guideposts softball team. And with each devotional, I learn something more about my relationship with God. I hope I can help you learn something too.

I will always be grateful that I wrote that first one. And in a way, I suppose, I'm still writing about guacamole, thanks to Van.

—Edward Grinnan

A Note from the Editors

The devotions in this book have been gathered from entries written by Edward Grinnan over a span of fifteen years. They have been organized into seasonal messages, which means that the timeline is not chronological. We hope you will find the selections for each season inspiring.

SPRING

Blessed is the man that trusteth in the LORD,
and whose hope the LORD *is.*
—JEREMIAH 17:7

THE BLESSING OF A BUSY DAY

May the favor of the Lord our God rest upon us; establish the work of our hands for us—yes, establish the work of our hands.
—PSALM 90:17 NIV

Spring has sprung in New York City, or more accurately *pounced*, with temperatures predicted to reach the eighties today and the nineties tomorrow. Debates about global warming aside, that's more like summer. Just last week the temperatures were dipping into the thirties at night, and folks were bemoaning what a cold spring we were having. My wife Julee left me a note on the fridge this morning, reminding me to clean the air conditioner filters.

Today I have a lot to do (in addition to those filters): Go to the gym, take winter clothing to the cleaners for storage (closet space is at a premium in New York City), pick up a few things for a business trip on Monday, pay bills (least favorite chore), take Millie to the dog park (most favorite chore) and pick up dog food (Millie's favorite chore), shop for groceries, drop car off for servicing. And since I haven't gotten to any of them yet, I'm feeling a sense of urgency verging on panic.

Yet in this season of getting things done, taking a minute to give thanks for the blessing of a busy day is not a bad idea. Yes, we all feel overwhelmed and hopelessly behind at times. There are moments when I feel I will never catch up. But the fact that there is so much for me to do—that my days are so packed with life—is a gift, a form of grace.

As hectic as things sometimes seem, God,
let me never forget that You are always at the center of my day.
Thank You for the gift of being busy.

****

WITH THE DOGS
IN CENTRAL PARK

To him that is joined to all the living there is hope.
—ECCLESIASTES 9:4

For a couple of energetic dogs living in a New York City apartment, Sally Brown, our three-year-old cocker spaniel, and Marty, our two-year-old yellow Lab, are pretty well-mannered. But they can be a handful, and then some.

Taking advantage of the weather one spring Saturday, my wife Julee, Sally, Marty, and I piled in a cab and headed up to Central Park. We were stalled in traffic when a horse pulling a carriage full of tourists stepped up and inclined its huge white head to the rear window of our cab. Marty came unstrung, howling and thrashing around the backseat. The terrified cabbie threw us out. I apologized and gave him a generous tip to make amends. He was smiling as we left him.

In the park, we took our eye off Sally just long enough for her to snatch a hot dog out of a little girl's hand. I bought the little girl another hot dog while Julee apologized to the mother. Meanwhile, the little girl gleefully fed her second hot dog to Marty. "She's always been afraid of dogs!" the mother said, laughing.

We then took the dogs to the lake near Bethesda Fountain for some swimming and fetching. That went fine until a wedding party, resplendent in white, came down the path. Naturally, Sally and Marty emerged from the murky waters to investigate the new arrivals and, of course, they had to shake out their sopping coats, splattering the bride and her maids with tiny dots of mud. Out of the corner of my eye, I saw Julee's lips moving in panicky prayer. All was well, though, and Marty and Sally ended up getting their picture taken with the bespattered bride. Somewhere, in some couple's wedding album, are two wet, grinning dogs, delighted to be part of the action.

A smiling cabbie, a slightly braver little girl, and an unusual wedding photo—not such a bad afternoon at that. Maybe God was teaching us, slyly using our two gregarious pets, to hone our skills as humans.

I am grateful, Lord, when You reach into my day
and train me how to handle life's stickier situations.

SPRING MEANS SOFTBALL

The streets of the city shall be full of boys and girls
playing in the streets thereof.
—ZECHARIAH 8:5

Spring may mean flowers to you, but for a fervent contingent here at the Guideposts editorial offices in New York City, spring means one thing: softball.

Our coed team formed a few seasons ago on something of a whim. No tryouts, no experience necessary; just a willingness to show up at East River Park under the shadow of the Williamsburg Bridge, play hard, and be entirely open to the possibility of making a fool out of oneself.

Our wise and courageous coach Stephanie made it clear that anyone who bought a uniform shirt was entitled to equal playing time. Many had never put on a glove before or swung a bat. The point wasn't to win, but to have fun.

It's a good thing the point wasn't to win. That first

season, we were woeful. Other teams discovered themselves beating us so badly that they declined to finish the game. That's called the mercy rule. We required a lot of mercy that first year. Yet we took delight in the few bright moments that occurred—one of George's towering home runs into the East River or Stephanie's speedy triples or just a fluky catch.

Undaunted, we turned out again the next season and won two games. Granted, one was a forfeit because our opponents couldn't find the field, but it counted as a "W" nonetheless. We gained a reputation for being scrappy. And we got better. Last season, we tied for first place and went to the city playoffs—the same team that could barely win a game our first year out.

The point still isn't to win. Just coming together and playing as a team was more fun than anyone imagined, and while we were having fun, we improved. To me, that's a tiny miracle.

Lord, as I dust off my glove for another softball season, keep me focused on fun. And let me not forget to be merciful, for there are games now when we're the ones who are called upon to exercise it, believe it or not.

READY TO SURRENDER

For when I am weak, then am I strong.
—2 CORINTHIANS 12:10

I was having lunch alone in a coffee shop, not really hungry and worrying again about my mother in a nursing home in Michigan, hundreds of miles away from rainy Manhattan.

Then Bob walked in. "Want some company?" he asked, shaking out his umbrella.

I was grateful to have him join me. Sometimes I slip up and say that my friend Bob beat a terrible drug and alcohol addiction. After all these years I should know better. "*I* didn't beat anything," Bob is quick to correct me. "It beat me. All I did was surrender."

I've learned a great deal from his sobriety, watching him rebuild his life into something far richer than he could have ever imagined when he was "out there." Nowadays Bob is a great success story, and he sees a spiritual solution to nearly every problem in life, big or small. He is always "letting go and letting God."

I, on the other hand, have trouble "surrendering." I don't always like to ask for help, not even from God. I'm usually trying to do it myself, to beat my problems, like my worries over my mother's Alzheimer's, even if it drives me crazy.

The subject of my mother never came up during lunch with Bob, but afterward I felt a whole lot better. I was ready to surrender.

Help me, God, to let go and let You.

URBAN FIREFLIES

For the eyes of the LORD run to and fro throughout the whole earth.
—2 CHRONICLES 16:9

From my street in Manhattan, I have a clear view of the Empire State Building. I love living beneath the once-tallest building in the world. Several other skyscrapers now surpass it, but to me it stills looks like the tallest building. It has that attitude. The colored floodlights illuminating its pinnacle change frequently. During Christmas, it's red and green; on the Fourth of July, red, white and blue; if the Yankees win the pennant, the lights go proudly to blue and white, the team's colors. Then there are the nights when the whole upper part is wrapped in cottony clouds.

Not long ago I noticed something curious. Tiny explosions of light were emanating from near the top of the Empire State Building, almost like urban fireflies. I'd never noticed them before. "Those are camera flashes," my wife Julee explained, "from people on the observation deck."

I had to laugh. The effective distance of a flash is only a few feet, certainly nowhere near enough to capture the sprawling panorama of the five boroughs and beyond, a vista that people from around the world come to behold. Back home, when they develop their film, it will be mostly black.

I suppose that should bother me a little bit, all that wasted flashing. It doesn't. I like knowing that there are people up there looking down at me, trying to take my picture. I like feeling part of a larger whole, a web of life that is too vast, too deep, and too textured to capture in the mere flash of a camera. It is a wondrous pattern that only the eye of God can take in all at once.

That's why, on a clear night, I always look up and check for that fusillade of camera flashes, just for the reminder of how much our lives on earth are connected in little ways that are part of a larger pattern that God has laid out. "Look," I say to Julee, "there go the fireflies."

I will always seek reminders, Lord,
of my place in Your world.

\#

JOY-FILLED SATURDAYS

*Blessed be the LORD, that hath given rest
unto his people Israel, according to all that he promised.*
—1 KINGS 8:56

Saturday. Who doesn't love that word? For me it means not just catching up on errands but also catching up on people. There's Arlene at the dry cleaners, who always can't wait to tell me how her son is doing in school (quite well), her voice bursting with maternal pride and gratitude. Hassan at my corner grocery fills me in on his family back in Egypt (some health problems, but they're doing all right now). Maria at the hardware store loves to be helpful ("We got that filter for your air conditioner, Mr. Grinnan"). And Cecil at the natural foods store is a *Guideposts* reader and is full of questions and comments about the most recent issue ("My wife loved that story about the little girl writing to the soldier in Iraq").

If I'm up in the Berkshires, Saturday might mean a climb up Monument Mountain or Mount Everett, or a day hike on the Appalachian Trail. Or maybe I just curl up on the couch with my dog Sally and watch a baseball game (I follow the Yankees, but just about any game will do) while my wife Julee leafs through catalogs.

Of course, Saturdays can also be hectic, and I often never get enough done. Still, after a long week of work, Saturdays are a way to reconnect not just with people but with the blessings of life. I think Saturday comes before Sunday to remind us of all that we have to be thankful for.

Lord, You fill my life with abundance and give me Saturdays to enjoy it so that on Sunday I come to Your house with a full and grateful heart.

Mother's New Family

Whosoever shall do the will of my Father which is in heaven,
the same is my brother, and sister, and mother.
—Matthew 12:50

I walked into my mother's room at Clausen Manor, where she is an Alzheimer's patient, to find her bed surrounded by people I thought were strangers. The night before, my sister had called me from Michigan. "You'd better come," she said, and I didn't have to ask why.

Mom looked unimaginably frail and parched. A woman with blonde hair held Mom's hand in both of hers while an aide dribbled sugar water from a dropper through Mom's lips, making rivulets of the deeper wrinkles on her chin. I noticed Mom's buddy Pat standing guard at the end of the bed. I now recognized the blonde woman, Colleen Burke, whom I'd met once not long after she'd taken charge of the unit. "Hey, green eyes," she said softly to Mom, "look who's here." My mother turned her head weakly and gave me that goofy Alzheimer's grin that had taken so much getting used to. The movement caused more sugar water to run down her chin as she made a sound that substituted for "Hi."

The hospice nurse and a social worker slipped in, and Mom's eyes brightened even as she tried to fend off the hovering dropper. "Hi, Estelle," whispered the nurse. Mom waved as if she were in a parade.

For an instant, I felt like an intruder. My mom had always been so profoundly devoted to her family. Yet here she was, dying, surrounded mostly by young strangers.

I made myself go forward. Colleen transferred Mom's hand to mine. Her grip was surprisingly strong, and she was pulling me closer even as she closed her eyes. I knew then that I was exactly where I was supposed to be, surrounded by my mother's new family, the people who cared for her on a daily, hourly basis. They were not strangers but helpers, and in the coming days I was to learn how much they cared.

*God, I thank You not only for the help You send
but for the people who bring it.*

###

"You Were Mom's Favorite!"

I prayed for this child.
—1 Samuel 1:27 niv

When my sister teased me on the phone the other day that I was always our mother's favorite, I was prepared to deny it, as usual. Yes, I was the baby of the family. And, yes, I came along late in my mother's life. Her "surprise," she liked to say. Still, I always thought my siblings made too big a deal of it. And after so much time, I would think they'd be tired of teasing me. I mean, we're all adults now.

Besides, parents may love their children differently but never one more than another. "Oh no," my sister always says, "you were the apple of her eye!"

Was that really true? My sister and I have talked about it a lot, and when we get serious, she always says that without me my mother would never have survived the death of my brother Bobby, the second youngest child, four years my senior. "You know, when Bobby died, if Mom hadn't had another little boy to love, I don't know what she would have done. You were her godsend."

My sister is right: My mother probably gave me enough love for two kids. In fact, maybe that's just what she was trying to do.

Father, You make a gift of us to others. Thank You for letting me be the little boy my mother needed to love twice as much.

****

OPENING DAY

For, lo, the winter is past, the rain is over and gone.
—SONG OF SOLOMON 2:11

T. S. Eliot may have had his reasons for thinking April was the cruelest month, but I always associate it with one glorious occurrence: Opening Day, when Major League Baseball gets its long, lumbering season under way, a season that will reach from the spring buds to the greening of summer grass through the kaleidoscopic fall. Baseball is one of life's great constants.

Baseball seems to follow me. I watched the historically dramatic game five of the 1975 World Series crowded around a fuzzy TV set in a tiny fishing village in Ecuador. My mom sent me the Detroit sports pages when I went East to school, so I could keep up with my beloved Tigers. And I remember being an impoverished freelance writer making my way to Yankee Stadium too broke to buy an Opening Day ticket but still wanting to eat a hot dog and watch the fans stream in.

My most vivid memory, though, is of one soft summer evening when I was a college student working as a deckhand on one of the big boats that haul iron ore across the Great Lakes. My ship, the *Roache*, was drifting down the Detroit

River. Sitting on a hatch cover, I felt a restless yearning as the Motor City skyline swept past. I'd been on the boat for most of the summer and I missed home. I missed the Tigers.

Tiger Stadium stood not far from the river. The lights were on. The evening was perfectly still, and the *Roache's* captain had cut the engines back because of the swift current. All at once I heard the stadium crowd roar, though it sounded more like a sigh at that distance, and a speck of white, like a tiny moon, arced above the rim of the stadium, through the wash of lights and high into the dusk, hanging suspended for an instant in the sapphire sky before falling back to earth, a routine fly ball. For that instant I felt a part of the crowd instead of alone on the deck of a freighter bound for Cleveland, and it felt good.

Every April on Opening Day, I remember that ball looping into a soft summer sky. God gives us many challenges in life, and sees us through many winters. But He also gives us baseball.

Thank You, Father, for the promise of spring.

CLIMBING MONUMENT MOUNTAIN

Come ye, and let us go up to the mountain of the LORD...
and he will teach us of his ways.
—ISAIAH 2:3

Once a year I make it a point to climb Monument Mountain in Great Barrington, Massachusetts. The views are impressive, and so is the lore connected with the rocky summit.

In 1850, two great American writers met there for the first time. Nathaniel Hawthorne hiked up the north side and Herman Melville ascended the south trail. They celebrated their rendezvous with a picnic lunch that was rudely interrupted by a tremendous summer thunderstorm. The authors took shelter in a cave, where they passed the time vigorously debating the great ideas of the day. Was mankind doomed to sin? Did science and technology offer a better future or were they to be feared? Could one man ever be allowed to oppress another?

The other day I made my annual pilgrimage. It was a warm day, but conditions improved a bit when the trail wound into the tree cover. I stopped to fill my water bottle from a quick-moving stream running down a crevice, then pushed on. Finally, I scrambled up some boulders to the top, where I could look out over the Berkshire Hills.

Melville and Hawthorne must have sat very near here and enjoyed their abbreviated repast. That reminded me. I pulled a sandwich out of my pack, ate slowly, and thought about the two writers. They had debated the great ideas of the day, and those questions hadn't changed very much in a century and a half. We still struggle with sin, science raises as many questions as it answers, and men continue to oppress other men, often horribly. And maybe that's what I needed to know: We continue to battle those ancient human failings, hoping that we become not a perfect race, but a better one in the sight of God.

Lord, I climb mountains so my ears can be a little closer to Your lips. Please help me to find answers.

##

"LIFE"
IN BRIGHT RED LETTERS

For with thee is the fountain of life:
in thy light shall we see light.
—PSALM 36:9

It was the end of another in a long string of hectic days, and I was leaving the office after dark again, exhausted, muttering that my wife Julee was going to kill me. I grabbed my briefcase and had just flipped off the lights in my office when I glanced out the window and saw the word *Life* emblazoned in the sky above Manhattan.

I stopped in my tracks. Maybe because I was so beat it took me a minute to figure out it wasn't a hallucination. No, the lit-up word was actually half of the MetLife logo atop its skyscraper ten blocks up the concrete-and-glass canyon of Park Avenue. Apparently the *Met* part had burned out, leaving just the word *Life* in bright red letters. Satisfied that the mystery was solved and that my sanity was reasonably intact, I started to leave again. I paused and looked back at the word suspended above the skyline. *Life.*

It hit me all at once, cutting through the headaches of the day. *What an incredible word! What an extraordinary concept!* The idea of being alive, of having life, seemed utterly startling, even improbable. We live in a universe made up of inert, nonliving matter and, overwhelmingly, empty space. We probe our galactic neighborhood for signs of life to no avail. As far as we know, life as we understand it exists only on this speck of rock and water and air we call earth. Life, against all odds, is ours. A cosmic gift.

It was getting late, and Julee was probably still going to

kill me. I was still feeling tired, still a little stressed-out, but most of all I felt alive.

Father, of all the gifts and blessings You bestow on us,
the greatest is the miracle of life. Let me find joy and satisfaction
in every amazing improbable moment.

##

MOM'S BUSY PRAYING

I cry to you for help, O Lord;
in the morning my prayer comes before you.
—PSALM 88:13 NIV

Is she there?" I asked Sherry, when my call bounced from my mother's room to the front desk. Sherry is one of the supervisors at the group home in Michigan where my mother, stricken with Alzheimer's, lives.

"She's praying with some of the other ladies," Sherry replied. It was a new Friday activity for the unit, along with shopping at a nearby mall and lunch at a popular restaurant.

Later, I got through to Mom in her room. "I called this morning," I said by way of reassuring small talk.

"Well, I must have been busy praying," Mom replied.

Strange, I mused, *that she should say that. Sherry must have just reminded her about those morning prayers*. Mom's illness forces her to live very much in the moment. She rarely remembers having spoken to me even fifteen minutes after the fact. When I call, she reacts with spontaneous joy, as if I am her long-lost prodigal son. Every conversation is a kind of reunion.

The next time I called on a Friday afternoon she said the same thing: "I was busy all morning praying."

Mom hadn't remembered the mall or the restaurant, so I asked Sherry about this mnemonic oddity. "Oh yes," Sherry assured me, "the one thing your mom never forgets is her prayers. We never have to remind her."

What can be crueler than a disease that steals our memories? My mother's mind is irreversibly eroding, like a sandy strip of beach being swept off by the charging surf, grain by grain. But prayer is a practice of the soul, an ongoing reunion with God. Mom has been in conversation with heaven for a long time. It helps me to know that her conversation continues, uninterrupted.

God, I will remember that prayer is a reunion with You.

SAYING, "I'M SORRY"

If we confess our sins, [God] is faithful and just,
and will forgive our sins and
cleanse us from all unrighteousness.
—1 JOHN 1:9 RSV

When I was little, my best friend was Mike Armstrong, the kid next door. One day after school, when we were playing a game, I got very upset with Mike for cheating. Alone in my room that night, I wished the worst things on him. Terrible things.

I awoke the next morning paralyzed with guilt. I knew what I had wished for Mike was a sin, and I had to tell it to a priest in confession. So that afternoon I went into my parish church, St. Dennis, and found a confessional that was lighted up.

The problem was I wasn't really sure of the exact name of the sin I had committed. Mentally, I ran my thumb down the Ten Commandments. There was one I didn't quite understand. *That must be it!* I decided by process of elimination.

When the priest slid open the confessional window, I got right down to business: "Bless me, Father, for I have sinned. Since my last confession I have committed one adultery."

Shocked silence.

This must be a really bad sin, I thought.

"How old are you, my son?"

"Eight, Father."

A soft chuckle drifted through the hush. Now what had I done? I was ashamed; I'd messed up my confession.

"Tell me about this sin," the priest prompted. All the terrible details of the things I'd wished on Mike came spilling out. I was crying when I finished.

The priest told me that what I had done *was* a sin, but not the one I cited. "The important thing is you're sorry," he reminded me, "and you are willing to be forgiven." For my penance, he told me to shake Mike's hand and apologize.

Good religion is also good advice. Today, when I am troubled by something I have said or done, even if I can't exactly put my finger on it, I remember that priest's words and I tell God I am sorry.

Father, I am willing to be forgiven.
Your perfect mercy is my saving grace.

HANDING OUT KEYS

Behold, God is my salvation; I will trust, and not be afraid.
—Isaiah 12:2

I'd walked almost all the way home when with a jolt of panic I realized I'd left my apartment keys in my desk drawer at work. My wife Julee was out of town. *Oh no....* It was starting to drizzle, and I had no interest in trekking back to my office. Then it occurred to me that my upstairs neighbor Anna kept an extra set of our keys for emergencies. Ricardo, our super, had a master set. And Ari, our next-door neighbor, still had the key we gave him when he watered our plants last time we were on vacation.

Suddenly, it struck me: *An awful lot of people can get into our place.* For instance, our new cleaning woman, Eva, and our previous one, Emily, who brought Eva over from their mutual homeland, Poland, when Emily finally got a job in her original field, biomedical technology. Then there was our dog walker, Sarajane, a veterinary student from England who worked at our vet's office, and her backup, Cara, an aspiring artist. There was Louie, Julee's musician friend, who sometimes stopped in to practice on our piano when no one was around. And Amanda, who occasionally availed herself of our spare bedroom when she was in town from Massachusetts. The more I thought about it, the more names came to mind of people who could let themselves into my home anytime they pleased. We'd been utterly profligate in handing out keys.

Was this such a bad thing? I wondered.

Perhaps. But I thought not. Every single person who had a key, I trusted completely. *What a terrible world this would be,* I decided as I walked up my street, *if I couldn't trust people.*

Anna and Ari were out to dinner (they'd left a note asking me to join them), and Ricardo was running an errand. Fortunately, Ricardo's sister Maria, newly arrived from the Dominican Republic, just happened to have let herself into his place with *her* extra set of keys, so when I knocked on the door she was able to show me where her brother kept mine.

Lord, thank You for making people trustworthy, and trusting.

\#

EPIPHANIES

And when they were come into the house, they saw the young child with Mary his mother, and fell down, and worshipped him.
—MATTHEW 2:11

The first time I heard the word *epiphany* used in a non-church context was in connection with the next-to-the-last scene of James Joyce's autobiographical novel *Portrait of the Artist as a Young Man,* which we were studying in our high school English class. I was curious to know why Joyce used the word to describe the dramatic episode in which the protagonist Stephen Daedalus at long last confronts his fate. "I thought the Epiphany referred to a feast day on the church calendar," I said to my teacher, who eyed me with his usual exasperation.

"Yes, Edward, but there's a secondary meaning to the word," he said, "which is the one Joyce intended in describing Stephen's personal epiphany on the beach. It means a startling insight, a realization or understanding that changes a person's life. A moment of inspired clarity."

Thinking back on it all these years later, I can't help wondering if my teacher misspoke by calling that definition secondary. Isn't it true that for every one of us, just as for the wise men who traveled so far from the East, the appearance of the Christ Child in our lives is a moment of inspired clarity that changes us forever? Christ can reveal Himself to us at any time and in an infinite number of ways. Whether they're little moments of grace or life-changing encounters, each and every one is an epiphany—in the fullest sense of the word.

Lord, as I live in your transforming light,
let this year be filled with
startling epiphanies and inspired clarity!

SEEING MY FATHER CRY

Jesus wept.
—JOHN 11:35

I saw my father cry only once. I was nine. It was a Saturday night at dinner. He was sitting at the head of our table talking quietly and distractedly about the terrible ordeal our family was undergoing. Bobby, my mentally retarded twelve-year-old brother, had been missing for several weeks; police feared the worst. In a few days, they would be proved right when the winter ice gave way to spring thaw and they found his body in a nearby lake.

But now my father still clung to some strand of hope. Suddenly, he stood up, almost toppling his chair. I think he wanted to get away from us. Instead, he smothered his face in his napkin and his whole body convulsed; then deep, speechless sobs filled the silence. I sat at the far end of the table, rigid. Tears dripped from my father's chin. Finally, I heard my mother whisper, "Oh, Joe..." and soon my father was silent. I tried to finish my dinner. For the first time in my life, my father seemed destructible, and it frightened me more terribly than my brother's disappearance.

A week later, at my brother's funeral, my father didn't cry. I had decided that I wouldn't either. All through the service I sat stiffly in the pew trying not to look at Bobby's casket at the foot of the altar, trying not to listen to what was being said, trying not to cry. At the cemetery, a chill Michigan wind snapped at the priest's robes as he sprinkled holy water on the descending coffin. When we got to the restaurant where thirty or forty of us gathered afterward, I was relieved to be out of the numbing spring cold, relieved it was over.

I looked around at the adults. They were hugging and crying, even the ones who like me had remained stoic throughout the long morning. Here they all were, their hearts overflowing, relieving their grief.

I found my big sister in the crowd. She was talking to an uncle. I wrapped my arms around her waist. I don't think she noticed as her wool skirt soaked up my tears.

Jesus wept, and in so doing
proclaimed His humanness.
Thank You, Father, for the gift of tears.

A BOUT OF INSOMNIA

The LORD's voice crieth unto the city.
—MICAH 6:9

I'm a little tired today. Last night I had one of my bouts of insomnia, worrying about a million things and nothing at all. Every stray sound became torture, and as anyone who's ever been to New York can attest, this is not a quiet city.

I turned on my air conditioner to muffle the noise outside. Desperate, I dug out some earplugs. No relief. *How will I function at work tomorrow? Lord, I need my rest!*

Suddenly, I found myself flashing back to the first time I ever spent the night in New York, years ago at a friend's apartment high above Park Avenue. I lay awake listening to the sounds of the streets drifting up. It was exciting, this concord of taxi horns, rushing subways, howling sirens, the general *swoosh* of traffic and the mingling of a thousand conversations. "It sounds just like the movies," I scrawled on a postcard home the next day, tired but feeling proud that I, a Midwestern exurbanite, had been baptized into the urban lullaby of New York.

The memory prompted me. I pulled out my earplugs, shut off the air conditioner and cracked the window. Then I lay back, listening, remembering, surrendering.

Yes, I'm tired today. Maybe I'll close my door this afternoon and steal a catnap at my desk, twenty-one floors above New York. Then again, maybe I'll just crack my office window and listen to God's tumultuous world in action and His voice in the din reminding me that life—even its noise—is a gift.

I must always try, Lord, to listen for You everywhere.

FEELING POOR

He who gives to the poor will lack nothing.
—Proverbs 28:27 NIV

I was feeling poor.

My wife Julee and I were walking west on Twenty-ninth Street through the April twilight after meeting with our accountant. We owed taxes. We owed our dentist for procedures not covered by insurance. We owed Marty's vet for treatment of an infected paw. Our savings were dipping. For the third month in a row we wouldn't be able to pay the full balance on our credit cards. And now we owed our accountant for giving us all this sorry news. "Where does all the money go?" I lamented.

Just off of Fifth Avenue we passed by a bedraggled young woman holding out an empty, fast-food coffee cup with a penciled dollar sign, the equal symbol, and the word *food* inscribed on it. Julee subtracted a wrinkled dollar bill from her jeans pocket and added it to the woman's cup. Shock prevented me from reacting for a few paces, then I exploded. "You know what she's going to spend it on!"

My wife shrugged. "Everyone has to eat. I like to think my dollar goes toward a meal."

I wasn't about to let her off the hook that easily. "Shouldn't we be worrying about our own money predicament?" I insisted. Then I got in a dig at the heart of Julee's habitual do-gooderism. "You're just doing it to make yourself feel better."

Julee stopped in her tracks. "Yeah," she agreed, "in a way I do. To be able to give something reminds me of how much I have, and that makes me feel blessed. So I guess I *am* making myself feel better."

I stood there on the dusky street, wondering if I looked

as stupid as I felt. I had let the scaly anxiety of our tax-time finances get the better of me, as I seemed to do every April. God would provide for us. He always does. Through Julee, He had even provided something in His own way for the young beggar.

I no longer felt so poor.

Lord, let me not forget that Your blessings are to be shared.

<hr>

ME AND TIGER STADIUM

Let the field be joyful, and all that is therein.
—PSALM 96:12

I flew to Detroit a few years ago to interview a ballplayer whose team would be playing that night at grand old Tiger Stadium on the corner of Michigan and Trumbull avenues. To me, the stadium was a shrine, not just to the Tigers and to baseball played on real grass under an open sky, but to a boyhood spent living and dying by the fortunes of the hometown team. How many sultry summer nights had I lain awake listening to Ernie Harwell describe one of Rocky Colavito's late-inning blasts arcing into the upper deck, kicking my feet in the air as Ernie shouted, "He's done it again, folks!"?

I arrived early and decided to wait out on the field. It was a nice spring day, the late-afternoon sun still high enough in the sky to bathe the infield in sunlight. There's nothing prettier than a major league infield, the grass cut short in crosshatch style, the dirt raked smooth and immaculately free of pebbles and debris. I marveled, thinking back to all those games I'd seen and listened to. I checked the clock above the scoreboard. A few of the ushers and vendors had drifted into the stands, preparing for the night's game.

Why not? I thought. This is my chance. I threw off my sport coat and ran to home plate. I made a mad dash down the first-base line, my wingtips kicking up the dust, rounded the bag, and chugged toward second. I touched second and headed to third, then steamed home, where I hit the dirt just under the imaginary tag. Springing breathlessly to my feet, I heard sporadic cheering and clapping from the bemused ushers. I waved heroically and pretended to tip my cap.

When I got back to the visitors' dugout, my interview subject had arrived and was giving me a perplexed look. But he just didn't understand. He got to do this every day.

> *Lord, thank You again for the blessing of baseball,*
> *for boyhood dreams and lifetime memories,*
> *and for moments in the sun,*
> *however brief and breathless.*

REMEMBERING MOM

Blessed are they that mourn: for they shall be comforted.
—MATTHEW 5:4

I had prayed for this to be just another day, but on the first anniversary of my mother's death I awoke to a wet and windy Saturday in the Berkshire Hills, the kind of raw early April morning that makes spring seem hopelessly far off. I'd wanted to hike a favorite stretch of the Appalachian

Trail, but the weather sabotaged my plans and I found myself wandering aimlessly through one of the musty secondhand bookstores for which this part of Massachusetts is known.

I needed another book like I needed a hole in my head, as Mom would have put it. I missed Mom saying things like that, missed them more than I ever imagined I would. I thought her long decline from Alzheimer's had prepared me for her death, but sometimes my feelings about losing her were unexpectedly poignant, like today.

As my eyes roamed the shelves, a title on a worn red spine leapt out at me: *The Southpaw's Secret*.

It was a boys' book, part of the relatively short-lived Mel Martin mystery series by John R. Cooper that I'd been crazy about when I was a kid. Mel Martin was a high school baseball star, and a crafty sleuth to boot. The books had already gone out of print by the time I read the two volumes I inherited from my older brother, but I was hooked. I don't know how many hours Mom spent helping me hunt down the other Mel Martin books.

Mom was a great sleuth herself, especially when it came to finding things for me: the Beatles' first album, for instance, which sold out the Monday after their historic appearance on *The Ed Sullivan Show*. Mom was able to unearth a copy in a tiny electronics store in Walled Lake, Michigan, about thirty miles from our house. Mom spent half her life finding obscure stuff I had to have.

Except *The Southpaw's Secret*, the one Mel Martin book she never was able to track down. And now it had found me. After all these years.

You are there, Lord, to help us find what we need.

##

BAD MORNING AT LAX

Be still before the LORD and wait patiently for him....
Do not fret—it leads only to evil.
—PSALM 37:7–8 NIV

The morning started badly. I slept through my wake-up call at my hotel in Los Angeles, leaving little time for the mad dash to the airport in the pouring rain. I nearly rear-ended a shuttle bus, trying to figure out how to work the rental-car phone so I could check on delays and see if there was any hope at all that I would make the meeting I had foolishly insisted on scheduling in New York that afternoon. Then I couldn't find the car return lot and ended up trapped in orbit around the airport. I finally spotted a sign that was obscured by construction equipment; I made a furious mental note to track down the people responsible and lodge a formal complaint when I got back home.

When I finally arrived at the lot and checked in, I missed the departing shuttle, then languished on the next one as the driver chitchatted with passengers. Is he trying to network a screenplay or something? Let's just get moving here! When he finally got around to putting the bus in gear and announced that my airline was the last stop on the run, I felt my mushrooming anger turn to despair.

I glanced around for another passenger who was as frenzied and desperate as I was, someone else whose existence was poised on the brink of chaos if all did not go precisely as planned. Everyone seemed quite relaxed, especially the man sitting across from me. He was reading his pocket Bible. A feeling of embarrassment and relief passed over me. He was doing what I had neglected to do—take a few minutes for

God. And here I was again, trying to control things only God can control, and driving myself temporarily insane.

I made my plane, I made my meeting, and most importantly, I made it home to my wife Julee and the dogs. But first, bouncing along on the rental car shuttle, I had closed my eyes and done what I should have done to begin with—found a few minutes for a God break.

Is it any wonder, Lord, that when I force myself ahead of You, my way becomes so difficult?

****

DAVID AND MIMI

He is our peace, who has made us both one, and has broken down the dividing wall of hostility.
—EPHESIANS 2:14 RSV

Shortly after I took over as editor-in-chief of *Guideposts*, we decided to give the magazine a makeover. We searched carefully for the right designer, someone who understood the soul of the magazine as well as the updated look we were after. That's how I met David Matt. He's from Virginia originally—*Guideposts* country to be sure—and his mother is a longtime subscriber. I made him promise to run his designs past Mom, so we'd have the opinion of a reader.

At the same time, we didn't want to neglect our *Angels on Earth* magazine. We hired one of the runners-up for the *Guideposts* job to help us revamp *Angels*. Her name is Mimi Park. Her parents are from Korea.

David and Mimi were colleagues. Well, more like

friendly rivals. Actually, not all that friendly. Mimi had wanted the *Guideposts* job, and she was determined to show us the error of our ways. David, for his part, had his considerable reputation to uphold. It worked out great for us as the two of them battled to outdo each other, always trying to sneak a look at the other's work.

It went on like that for months until the projects were completed and we had a little party to celebrate the success of the redesigns. It was there that we noticed David and Mimi off in a corner by themselves, spending an inordinate amount of time in conversation.

Do I have to tell you what happened? Last year, David and Mimi were married, and this year David redesigned *Daily Guideposts* for us. David and Mimi are part of the family now, and I shouldn't be surprised. Because that's what Guideposts—its magazines, its books, its Web sites and outreach—is all about: bringing people together.

Lord, You bring us together from all over to tell people
about Your grace. The closer we are to each other,
the closer we are to You.

SARAH HAVING A BAD LIFE

"Nevertheless not my will, but thine, be done."
—LUKE 22:42 RSV

Until my friend Sarah called, I thought I was having a bad day. The things I wanted to happen at my office weren't happening—at least not the way *I* wanted them to—

and all morning I had been shooting God what could only be called metaphysical dirty looks. Then the phone on my desk burbled.

Had Sarah not identified herself, I never would have recognized her voice. She was crying. "I just needed to call someone," she said.

"Bad day?" I asked.

"Bad life," she retorted. I knew through our mutual good friends that Sarah's mother was gravely ill, and that her job had changed, and that she and her fiancé had recently postponed their wedding. My own problems began to shrivel.

"What happens," she wanted to know, "if the things you hope for most in your life, the things you've dreamed about since you were little, are not part of God's plan for you?"

It was not a question I was prepared for in the middle of a busy workday, and I groped for something reassuring to tell Sarah. But while I was fumbling with a well-meant platitude, she interrupted me and answered her own question. "I guess the thing I have to pray for is to accept God's will for me."

I knew Sarah well enough to know that she really didn't believe that she was having a bad life, and that when she hung up the phone she would do exactly what she said: Say a prayer of acceptance rather than a prayer of demand. What she probably didn't know was that because of her call, I would be praying the same prayer.

God, You made me flexible so that I can bend.
I must remember: Thy will, not mine.

MOTHER'S DAY

My son...forsake not the law of thy mother.
—PROVERBS 1:8

A few years ago, after my mother moved into a nursing home, I spent a melancholy weekend boxing up her things, trying to decide what should be saved and what should be tossed out, and resisting the urge to donate it all to Goodwill and let them deal with it.

Then, in the big bottom drawer of her old oak wardrobe, I discovered a collection of stuff in a beat-up Hudson's department store box: all the childhood gifts I'd given her for Mother's Day. I didn't know whether to cringe or cry.

There was the shamrock key chain with the illegible "Mom" I engraved on it myself, and the Jean Naté Fleur de Versailles bath set I saved my lawn-mowing money to buy at the five-and-ten. She still had the awful blue Wedgwood candy dish with the poodle head cameo in honor of Pete, our dog. There was the pot holder that said "#1 Cook" (Mom didn't really like to cook); a chintzy picture frame with my fifth-grade class shot still in it, taken the day after I got a front tooth knocked out playing tetherball; a snow globe of the Mackinac Bridge from my smart-aleck gag-gift phase (crossing that huge span always made her dizzy); and the cards with my earnest attempts to put my feelings into words. I was amazed I ever passed spelling, let alone penmanship.

Yet what I felt most keenly as I went through those Mother's Day gifts of mine was the joy with which each and every one was received, the delight Mom took in the act of giving, especially when practiced so imperfectly by a little boy. No, Mom never cringed, not even at the sight of the

Wedgwood poodle dish, and sometimes, I remember, she did cry. So did I that day over the old Hudson's box. No one will ever love you like your mother, they say, and I had found proof of that.

Lord, You give us mothers for countless reasons.
I think the most important is this: They teach us to love.

"MILLIE!"

Take hold of the eternal life to which you were called.
—I TIMOTHY 6:12 RSV

Millie, my golden retriever puppy, is asleep on her bed in front of a woodstove on a chilly spring night, totally tired as only a busy puppy can be. Earlier in the day she had her first visit to my office. Then it was into the Jeep for the three-hour ride to our house in western Massachusetts, Millie's first visit there too. She was a little carsick on the way up, and the look on her face when we finally parked in the driveway was like someone who had just gotten off a wild amusement park ride. As soon as she hit the ground, though, she was off like a shot, tearing down the hill out back, right for the woods.

"Millie!" I yelled.

Coyotes, bears, mountain lions...skunks!

"Millie!"

All the books say not to run after a puppy; they like being chased. Stay still and call them. I immediately ran after her.

"Millie!"

She made a sharp right turn into a neighbor's yard and raced around to the back porch where she encountered a black Lab named Simon through the kitchen window. Simon came out, and they played and chased for the next hour until they both dropped from exhaustion. I gave Millie some extra treats with dinner that night, and now, here she was, snoring gently by the stove, as oblivious to the world as can be.

And all at once I want to freeze everything in time—this moment, this day, Millie's gentle breathing, this incredible feeling of peace and contentment that has swept over me. I want to grab that feeling and hold it so tight I will always remember what this moment feels like. I don't want time ever to move again because I would be perfectly happy living in this moment forever.

Thank You, God. Thank You for these incredible moments of bliss and grace, these little glimpses, it would seem, of heaven itself.

##

BASH BISH FALLS

Hath not my hand made all these things?
—ACTS 7:50

There is a spot I like to hike to in the Berkshire Hills of western Massachusetts called Bash Bish Falls. Over the west shoulder of Bash Bish Mountain forks a riot of white water that, cleaved by a granite promontory, sluices down in two twisting, tumbling midair streams to a deep, mossy pool a hundred feet or so below, producing the sound that has become its name.

I head for Bash Bish whenever I need a chance to get

away and think. By the time I reach the trailhead above the falls, breathing hard, I've begun to feel peaceful, yet more alive to the world, my senses pricked by the air and sky and water.

But not on this day. I come to Bash Bish feeling at odds with the world for no particular reason, just a little uncertain as to how I fit into it all. Forlorn, I crouch on a big, flat rock and stare down at the falls. I hear a rustle along the trail, and out pops a woman with a thick nest of once-red, now graying hair, making her way slowly but steadily with the assistance of a tall, crooked walking stick. She reaches the edge of my rock, stops and turns toward the falls. We are silent, except for our breathing, which is soon absorbed by the sound of the falls—*bash bish, bash bish*. We stay that way long enough for me to be aware of the sun sinking. Then the woman says, to no one in particular, "Well, if He can take care of all this, then He can surely take care of me." With that she's off, heading down the other side of the trail, first her head and then the crooked tip of her walking stick dropping slowly from sight.

I stay a bit longer on my rock before racing the sun down the mountain. I just want to get one last look at how I fit into it all.

Lord, You make a place for me in Your beautiful world.
Surely You will not forget me.

SUMMER

Be of good courage,
and he shall strengthen your heart,
all ye that hope in the LORD.
—PSALM 31:24

LIGHT OF THE WORLD

And the light shineth in darkness;
and the darkness comprehended it not.
—JOHN 1:5

More than a half million visitors come annually to see the Book of Kells at Trinity College, Dublin, and my hotel's concierge encouraged me to go have a look. "Ah, 'tis a lovely thing to see, sir," he said, pointing me in the direction of Trinity.

The Book of Kells, dating from AD 800, is a copy of the four Gospels. It was painstakingly transcribed and illuminated—that is, illustrated—by the monks of St. Columba on the island of Iona before it was removed to Kells in County Meath to protect it from plundering Vikings.

My eyes took a while adjusting to the dim lighting of the Old Library's East Pavilion where the manuscript is kept. There were only a few tourists, but there were several groups of Irish schoolchildren, and I kept bumping into them in the russet gloom. "It's so dark in here I can hardly see my own foot," I remarked to a studious-looking older gentleman bent over one of the display cases.

"Light can damage the paper," he remarked. "None at all would be best, but then..." His words trailed off as he gestured to the milling children. My eyes followed his back to the fragile but magnificent pages beneath the glass, bathed in soft light. The breathtaking beauty of the manuscript shone through as if it had light of its own.

The monks labored over their manuscript during what we call the Dark Ages. Their rich and ornate embellishments emblazoned the pages of Scripture, the words of Jesus that lighted the way through the chaos and darkness that followed the fall of the Roman Empire. All these centuries later, we are protecting the Light of the World from—literally—the light of the world.

We may not consider ourselves as living in a dark age, but you never know. One Light burns a path of beauty and brightness when all seems dark. And it burns brightest when the world seems darkest.

Lord, Your Word is our light.

ALWAYS GIVING DIRECTIONS

Trust in the LORD with all thine heart;
and lean not unto thine own understanding.
In all thy ways acknowledge him,
and he shall direct thy paths.
—PROVERBS 3:5–6

One of my favorite cartoons depicts a hardhearted Manhattanite glaring at a tourist who is sheepishly asking, "Can you tell me how to get to the Statue of Liberty or should I just get lost?"

I am just the opposite. I love giving directions. And I don't just give vague, generalized directions, either. I like to be as specific as possible and sure of my information. The more exact I can be, the more satisfaction I take in rendering assistance and the more confident I feel that the person will get where he or she is going.

This all amuses my wife to no end, perhaps because

she's spent so many hours sitting in the passenger seat of a car while I drive around completely lost, yet refusing to get directions. "Why can't you just stop and ask someone?" she'll demand. But that would be too easy. It isn't a matter of stubborn male pride—or at least I don't think it is. It's more a sense that I want to figure things out for myself. There is, of course, a point at which I should just admit defeat and ask someone for help. But that point doesn't come easily for me.

All of which leads me to ask myself a question: Am I like that in my prayer life too? Always giving directions— "Lord, grant me this" and "Father, help me to do that"— instead of seeking them? I listen to myself pray sometimes and it's more like I'm placing an order. So here's my new resolve: Ask for direction.

That's me, God, the guy who's lost and still won't ask You for help. Next time I am in a bind, I'll try asking for direction instead of giving it.

##

HAVE A NICE DAY?

The LORD is nigh unto all them that call upon him.
—PSALM 145:18

I think of myself as pretty good-natured, but every so often, I have one of those days.

It happened yesterday. First, it was the well-meaning guy at the market feeding my dogs Marty and Sally pieces of stale bagel while I was trying to gather milk and the morning papers. "Stop it!" I snapped, struggling to untangle Sally's leash from around my ankle. "It's not good for them."

I wasn't much nicer to my building super, who'd promised to fix my dripping bathroom faucet. "It's driving me nuts," I growled as I came into the lobby. "I can hardly sleep at night!"

I let loose an irritated sigh when a delivery boy wedged himself into the elevator as the door was closing. Of course, he started paying attention to the dogs, and again I was ensnared in leashes.

I dropped my keys trying to unlock my apartment, the metallic splash jangling my nerves even more. "Have a nice day," a neighbor leaving for work sang out.

"If you insist."

It was everything I could do not to slam the door behind me. *Have a nice day?* I was having a horrible day, and it had barely started. And the longer it went on like this, the worse it would get and the more miserable I would feel.

"All right, God," I said, giving in. "I know it's up to me. At least I can try to have a nice day instead of trying to have a bad one. But let's not kid ourselves—I need Your help."

Did I have a nice day? Not exactly. But I didn't have the terrible day I was initially bent on having. Whenever I felt myself giving in to irritation, I mentally took a step back and asked God to take over. Time and again, He handled situations I couldn't. Sometimes, I learned, He is nearest when I am at my worst.

You make all my days good, Lord, even when I'm not.
I'll try a little harder next time—with Your help.

TONY AND MILLIE

There is no fear in love; but perfect love casteth out fear.
—1 JOHN 4:18

Julee and I have owned four dogs since we've lived in our Manhattan apartment building, and our neighbor Tony has been terrified of every one of them—until Millie. Not that our other dogs were vicious; no, it was Tony. He had a lifelong fear of dogs. Even when our cocker spaniel Sally was hobbling around with arthritis, Tony refused to get in the elevator with us. The mere sight of Marty, our hundred-pound Labrador retriever, was enough to make Tony go weak in the knees. "I don't hate your dogs," Tony tried to explain from a safe distance. "I'm just afraid of them."

For years I tried to keep our dogs away from Tony, pulling them back when we crossed paths with him in the lobby, crossing to the other side of the street when we saw him outside. Then came Millie, our now-three-year-old golden retriever. If you've ever known a golden, you know that they are the sweetest creatures God has created.

During their first couple of encounters, I tried to pull my big puppy back from Tony as he retreated in terror. Millie wasn't having it. She sat down politely, tail swishing on the floor and waited for Tony to pass. Then when they met, she tried to approach him, head down, moving slowly, but determined to show him she was a friend. One day he put his hand out tentatively and patted Millie on the head. Millie was thrilled. Tony couldn't believe he'd done it. "Wow!" was all he could say.

Nowadays Tony gets down on one knee to give Millie a bear hug while she nuzzles his neck. And you know what? Tony stopped me the other day and asked, "Can you recommend a good place to adopt a dog?"

It's only fair, I guess. A dog already adopted him.

God, Your love abides in many forms—
some four-legged—that bring joy to the heart.
Thank You for the time we have with them.

##

MOM AND THE
BENT STEAK KNIFE

He giveth grace unto the lowly.
—PROVERBS 3:34

Growing up, I remember an inexpensive set of steak knives with plastic handles meant to look like wood. There was one that was bent, its handle heat-warped by the dishwasher. By decree of some sort, Saturday night was steak night at our house, and you knew it by the fact that Mom set the table with the steak knives. Invariably, the bent one was at her place. Typical mother behavior, I always thought.

The number of table settings diminished through the years as my siblings grew up and moved out—I am the youngest—yet every Saturday, the same humble, deformed utensil would appear at Mom's place. When I teased her about always choosing the bent knife, she would say she felt sorry for it, the way I suppose she felt sorry for household spiders whom she'd scoop up in her hand and sneak outside before my father could dispatch them with a rolled-up section of the *Detroit Free Press*. It's true, Mom always loved the underdog.

Shortly before we had to move her into an Alzheimer's unit, a number of years after my father died, I showed up while she was eating dinner alone in that house once so full of children. It wasn't steak night, but, yes, at her place setting was the old bent-handled knife.

Typical mother behavior? Maybe. But Mom certainly wasn't egoless; far from it. She was proud, fiercely proud, of many things: her family; her children; her own sharp, restless, independent mind. She was known to brag a bit, that is true. But as I grew older I understood how hard my mother worked at practicing humility. She saw humility as a *spiritual* discipline, a redemptive one, a reminder of her role in God's world. After all, this was the woman who walked around on Good Friday with a sharp pebble in her shoe to remind her of Christ's suffering. No doubt that knife reminded her of something too: that even in our smallest, humblest choices we can honor God.

Teach me, God, a lesson in humility,
a lesson in serving You.

OF SHIRT STAINS AND BUTTERFLIES

He has made everything beautiful in its time.
—ECCLESIASTES 3:11 NIV

This morning I dressed in the dark so as not to disturb my wife Julee, who was sleeping in after a late-night singing gig. Imagine my dismay when I arrived at work only to discover a small, ugly stain on my fresh shirt, a stain my neighborhood laundry had vowed to banish. It was virtually unnoticeable, I'm sure, but immediately I imagined that no one who came in contact with me could possibly ignore my blighted appearance. Later at a meeting, I felt utterly self-conscious. At some point I must have told myself, *Look, you're being silly*, but it did no good.

It was a lovely Manhattan day. A bright summer sun bleached the skyscrapers. I was walking from lunch across West Thirty-second Street with a friend when I detected people staring at me. Yes, I was certain someone pointed. I reminded myself to demand a refund from the laundry. Then I noticed my companion grinning. "You'll never believe this," she said.

"What?" I was growing tense.

"There's a big, beautiful butterfly riding on your shoulder."

Out of the corner of my eye, I made out a pulsating smear of color, ocher and orange and blue.

"Careful," she whispered, "you might scare it off."

But it wasn't going anywhere, at least not anywhere I wasn't going. All the way across Thirty-second Street, west to east, the butterfly perched on my shoulder like a cool flame, and everywhere people stared and pointed and smiled.

"How did you teach him to do that?" one astonished kid asked.

The butterfly stayed with me for a good fifteen minutes, the entire way back to my office building, before fleeing the arctic air conditioning of the lobby. "That was amazing!" my friend said.

Amazing, certainly. But not as amazing as God, who gives me a nudge when I'm thinking foolishly, and shows me that He made people far more interested in beauty than in ugliness.

Thank You, Lord, for stains and butterflies
and sunny days—for everything.

##

A VOICE SAID,
"GO TO YOUR FRIEND VAN"

I, even I, am he that comforteth you.
—ISAIAH 51:12

I pointed my rental car eastward through the early morning clouds draping the San Francisco Bay Bridge. I was rushing out to a hospital in San Pablo to see my friend Van, who had collapsed from a stroke a few days before while waiting to board a cruise ship bound for New Zealand. His friend Daniel and nephew Gordon reported that he was in bad shape. I thought I might wait until they brought Van back to New York City, but a voice said, *No, you must go to him.*

What if he didn't know me? What if he was completely unresponsive? The mere thought of Van, one of my oldest and dearest friends, not even recognizing me was devastating; the thought that he might die, unthinkable.

I parked my car in the crowded hospital lot. Every step toward the entrance was an effort. I was afraid—afraid to face the worst. I wanted to turn back. *God, please help me do this.*

Van was alone when I got to his room. I spoke to him. No response. I leaned over and looked at his eyes. Closed.

His mouth was open and his breathing ragged. My worst fears were coming true, and somewhere deep inside me a sob began to form, one I knew that I'd never be able to hold back. I slipped my hand around his. "Van..."

And I felt it, all the way up through my arm: Van's strong, hard grip. I felt it all the way to my heart. Then he pulled my hand to his lips and held it there for a long moment.

He didn't open his eyes or even move his head. He didn't speak. But he didn't need to.

Dear God, You guide us through the fog of our deepest emotions
and give us clarity when all seems dark and hopeless.
With You there is always comfort.

A MEMBER OF THE KOREAN LADIES CLUB

So we, being many, are one body in Christ,
and every one members one of another.
—ROMANS 12:5

The gym I go to in the morning is situated on the fringes of Manhattan's Koreatown, a bustling center of commerce and entertainment. After my workout, if I have the time, I repair to the pool area to baste in the sauna and percolate in the whirlpool. That's where I see them: a half dozen or so middle-aged Korean ladies who keep up a constant stream of banter in their native tongue. I usually mind my own business and stay out of their way, but it makes me happy to know that they're there.

The other morning when I slipped into the sauna, the Koreans burst into laughter. I spread my towel on the bench as usual. *Were they laughing at me?* I tried to give them a smile back, but I'm sure it came out more like a grimace. I sat down and the giggles subsided.

Later, showered and dressed for work, I ran into a couple of the ladies in the elevator, likewise prepared for the day. One of them told me, "We laughed because we had just been discussing whether or not you would appear, then you showed up. You are like one of the club."

For a while I'd watched them interact. I'd seen them massage each other's tired shoulders, share lotion, and give each other hugs. One morning when the terror alert in New York City had been elevated, I watched them form a prayer circle. I don't understand a word of Korean, yet I know that these women share a profound bond of friendship. I know that they care deeply about each other.

And now I am a member of their club.

Father, thank You for the blessing of friends and community,
and for the Korean Ladies Club, of which,
I recently learned, I am an official member.

##

WHEN JULEE LOST HER MOM

Then shall be brought to pass the saying that is written,
Death is swallowed up in victory.
—1 CORINTHIANS 15:54

My wife Julee and her mom Wilma Cruise were extraordinarily close. No matter where Julee was in the world—and it could be anywhere—she called her mom in Creston, Iowa, every day without fail. Even after Wilma's capacity for speech was pretty much wiped out by a stroke, Julee was the one person who managed to carry on conversations with her. The nursing home would call Julee when they couldn't figure out what Wilma wanted; somehow Julee always knew.

Wilma died this year, very peacefully. I did everything I could for Julee as she sank deeper into mourning. I tried to get her to eat, to exercise, to make it to her doctor's appointments. I told her that God was with her no matter how alone she felt, that He was really there, closer than ever. I sat up with her late into the night, sometimes without even talking. But still she grieved.

Finally, in frustration and despair, I told a friend there was nothing more I could do. "I feel so inadequate," I said.

My friend looked at me for a long time, then said simply, "It's death. We're supposed to feel inadequate."

We humans can overcome just about anything, but we can't overcome death. And the deeper we love, the harder we grieve. Finally we come through the other side, as I know Julee will, when our love becomes acceptance— perhaps of our own inability to let go of people all at once. We don't want to let go, so we let go in stages— imperfect, painful, not always pretty. And each and every step of the way God takes hold of what we have let go.

Only You, eternal Lord,
can turn death into eternal life.

MARLA AND GOOD, HEALING PAIN

Christ also suffered for you, leaving you an example,
that you should follow in his steps.

—1 PETER 2:21 RSV

Marla was one of the kindest, gentlest, most compassionate people I'd ever met, which made it all the more dismaying that she was so intent on causing me pain. Marla was my physical therapist after I broke my arm last year playing softball. Her office was across the street from mine, so I made my thrice-weekly appointments for early in the morning before work.

The first couple weren't so bad. She kneaded my arm and stretched it a bit while we chatted amiably. *This person wouldn't hurt a fly*, I reassured myself. Then, the second week, we got down to business. Marla would slowly twist my arm in one direction and murmur, "Tell me when it hurts."

"Yow!" I'd yelp.

But rather than stopping, she would twist it further.

"Yow!"

Then she would hold it there.

"Count to three," she'd say in her soft, soothing voice. I'd make it to three in record time.

"What you are feeling," Marla explained, "is good pain. Healing pain. You get better by going through it, not around it. It's the only way." Still, as the weeks passed, more and more I found myself playing hooky from PT.

It was during this time that I lost my mother after a long battle with Alzheimer's. When all the postmortem rituals were done, I was left in a kind of emotional fogbank, trying not to dwell on the darkening pain. I put in longer hours at the office and pushed myself harder at the gym. Then Marla called. "I haven't seen you for a while," she said. "Don't you want to get better?"

Her question was still running through my thoughts as I lay on the therapy table the next morning. Marla carefully manipulated my arm, tugging it in a direction I swore it would not go. When she said to count to three, I did—slowly. It was the only way.

Lord, teach me to trust You to be my guide from the darkness to Your eternal light, step by sometimes painful step.

###

ANSWERED PRAYER FOR MY CAR TROUBLE

In every thing by prayer and supplication with thanksgiving let your requests be made known unto God.
—PHILIPPIANS 4:6

It sounded like a sick animal had taken up residence under the hood of my car that Monday morning when I started it up. *Oh no.* For a kid from Detroit, I know pathetically little about the mechanics of an automobile.

I stared at the incomprehensible array of gauges and indicator lights in the dashboard. Nothing seemed awry. Just this racket emanating from the engine. *Maybe it'll go away*, I thought desperately.

As I drove to the store to pick up a few things, I found myself begging God, "Look, I don't want to take the car into the shop this week. *Please* help me out." As soon as I said the prayer, I was embarrassed by the smallness of it. What kind of problem was this to bother the Creator of the universe with? I decided that if the engine was still bellowing when I started up the car again, I'd bite the bullet and take it in to the shop.

I bought the things I came for and returned to the car. I took a breath. I turned the key.

Ffrrumphakatatata...

I leaned my forehead against the steering wheel. *No telling what it will cost—parts, labor, tax....*

"Hey!"

I looked up. A man was tapping on my windshield. "Sounds like your power steering fluid is low," he said. "Better check it out." Then he was gone.

I turned off the engine, jumped out and took a look. I located the power steering fluid reservoir and checked the level. He was right! At least, I hoped he was. I ran back inside the store and inquired about fluid. Sure enough, they had shelves of it at a price so low I found it hard to believe. A few minutes later, the engine was purring like a warm kitten.

All right, Lord, You win again. Who am I to say what prayers are important and what aren't? And thanks for the tip about the power steering stuff.

✳✳

REGRETS FOR
NOT STAYING IN TOUCH

A devout man...prayed to God always.
—Acts 10:2

Back when I was cooling my heels between college and graduate school, stubbornly without plans for the future,

I lit out on a long, vagabond adventure that took me from the mountains of Ecuador to the Amazon River basin of Peru and Colombia to the shores of Lake Titicaca in Bolivia. It was rare that I would find time to sit down and drop my mom a line. When I *did* write, I told her how at the little rural hotel where I was staying you had to inspect your shoes every morning for tarantulas. Or that guerrillas had menaced our bus in the remote Colombian countryside. One of the few times I phoned was to report that I was laid up in a La Paz hospital with dysentery. "Don't worry," I said, "they've decided it's not cholera."

My poor mother. I'd tortured her without meaning to. Like so many young adults, I had mistaken self-centeredness for self-awareness, recklessness for freedom. One day on the phone I asked her, "Do you remember when I was lost in South America?"

"Of course I do," she snapped. Even Alzheimer's hadn't erased that memory.

"I'm sorry I didn't keep in touch more, Mom. I know it worried you."

"Oh, I was frantic most of the time!" she agreed, as always clearer about the past than the present. "I prayed like the dickens. Everywhere you went, my prayers went with you."

I thought more about that after we hung up. My mother had had a powerful secret weapon, and so had I without knowing it. Like a passport, prayers go with us wherever we go, across all borders and around the world, to keep us safe and to bring us home.

Father, forgive me when I fail to keep in touch
and remind me that wherever I go, You go.

LONNIE AND FLUFFY

He hath put a new song in my mouth, even praise unto our God.
—PSALM 40:3

My neighbor Lonnie is quite a character. Ask her what kind of day she's having and get ready for an earful. Shopkeepers roll their eyes and neighbors sometimes avoid her. She has a good heart, really. It's just that she can be so negative sometimes. I don't think she even realizes she's doing it.

So everyone was surprised a while back when Lonnie appeared walking a fluffy little dog by the name of...Fluffy. The dog had been given as a companion to a sick relative of Lonnie's, but the relative had grown too ill to care for it. "So it looks like I'm stuck with him!" she said.

Fluffy was a good dog but not used to a leash, so there was a lot of pulling and tugging between Lonnie and Fluffy. Lonnie was frustrated, and the dog was confused. "Bad dog, Fluffy!" I would hear Lonnie shouting at him, with Millie, my golden retriever, looking on in disapproval. No, Lonnie and Fluffy were not a happy pair. Finally someone recommended a dog trainer to Lonnie.

The trainer joined Lonnie and Fluffy on their morning walks. "Lonnie," she preached, "positive reinforcement is what's most effective. Praise good behavior, ignore bad, and never lose your patience or act negative. Never say *bad* and always praise."

Praise? I don't think I'd ever heard such a thing come out of Lonnie's mouth. Yet soon enough, there she was on the street with Fluffy, saying "Good dog, good dog!" in the "happy voice" the trainer taught her whenever Fluffy complied with proper leash etiquette. Soon enough, Fluffy was walking like a champion.

Lonnie and Fluffy are now inseparable. There's something

else too: Lonnie's not quite so grumpy anymore. She lights up when people stop to admire Fluffy, and she's not so quick to go negative during a conversation. Giving praise has changed her.

Father, a positive attitude is one of the greatest spiritual gifts. Help me to remember: Praise! Praise! Praise!

IN THE WEE HOURS, SCREECHING TIRES AND PRAYER

We know not what we should pray for as we ought: but the Spirit itself maketh intercession for us.
—ROMANS 8:26

I awoke at 4:15 this morning, praying urgently to the sound of screeching rubber, crashing metal, and shattering glass. I was completely alert, anxious even. I'd been praying when I woke up, a split-second before I heard the skidding tires. *Lord, help those people in the accident. Be with them. Comfort them.*

This is New York; I'm used to being awakened at all hours by the city that never sleeps (and sometimes won't let you, either). Still, I couldn't remember ever waking up actually praying.

Even now, I didn't want to stop.

There was an all-night newsstand on the corner; they would surely call the police. Beat by beat, my heart rate decelerated from a gallop to a canter. My wife Julee slumbered peacefully beside me, her slow breathing mingling in the dark with the dogs' tranquil snores. Finally, I drifted back to sleep to the sound of voices and approaching sirens.

A few hours later, I was buying my morning paper on my way to the office. "What on earth happened out here last night?" I asked Hassan, the newsdealer.

He paused, then nodded. "Oh yes, that. Just a little fender bender. Nothing to worry about."

I strode across the intersection, now clogged with commuter traffic. My eye caught a few shards of a brake light glittering in the morning sun, the only evidence of any kind of mishap. I found myself resenting having been awakened so dramatically for a mere fender bender.

Yet the urgency of that prayer still echoed. I'd awoken an instant before I heard the screeching tires, and I was already praying. What did it mean?

I reached the other side of the intersection. Maybe I wasn't meant to know. The accident certainly sounded as if someone could have been hurt. What I knew for sure was that I felt as if I'd been shaken awake and told, "I need you."

God, thank You for those extraordinary moments when You use me to help others. Let me always be ready, even in the dead of night.

##

SEPTEMBER 10, 2001

Lo, I am with you alway, even unto the end of the world.
—MATTHEW 28:20

September 11 is a date whose imprint on our national consciousness will take generations to fade. But it's September 10 that stays with me somehow. It's just the other side of a line of demarcation, perhaps the last day of an era.

September 10, 2001, was a perfect late-summer day, like the infamous day that would follow. New Yorkers went about their business, absorbed by the daily trials and rewards of life in the city. I took a good friend to lunch for her birthday. We groused that the restaurant had run out of the crab cakes we'd wanted to order. How could they? The baseball pennant races were on, important enough to make the front pages of the tabloids. The last thing I did that day at work was to make plane reservations for a business trip the following week. I didn't give it a second thought. Why should I?

Since then, nothing has been quite the same. But on that September 10—on any day of my life, really—I could not possibly have known what the future held. I am not given that knowledge. That's what stays with me about this day, haunts me even—the complete uncertainty of tomorrow.

Yet I am given a knowledge far greater than the ability to see the future. I know, with the utmost certainty, that whatever unlooked-for events the next day may bring, God is with me, today, tomorrow, and forever.

> *Lord, Your love and protection is the one true thing*
> *that I can count on. It's always ahead of me,*
> *guiding my way through all uncertainty.*

###

FIVE FEET
SEVEN-AND-A-HALF INCHES

Which of you by taking thought can add one cubit unto his stature?
—MATTHEW 6:27

The news from my doctor was bad.

"Five-seven," he said, studying the height scale during my annual physical.

"And a half," I lobbied.

"All right, I'll give it to you."

Still, it was an inch shorter than the last time my height was checked way back in my twenties. My weight I tracked scrupulously, but I had never bothered with height. I knew I was five feet eight-and-a-half inches tall (and that half inch meant a lot). Why would that ever change? "Our spines compress," my doctor said breezily as I dressed. "It's a natural part of aging. You're fortunate. Count your blessings." He sent me on my way. I called my wife immediately and told her the grim news.

"Don't scare me like that!" Julee barked. "I thought for a second something was really wrong." Then she pretty much hung up on me.

Could I blame her? I was being totally silly. And vain. That's what this was about—vanity. And I disliked catching myself being vain, disliked it even more than my shrinkage.

Hustling down the sunny street toward the subway, I took a second and looked around me. The street was full of people, all sorts of people, all sorts of colors and sizes and styles and ages. No two of them were alike. And it was wonderful. It was beautiful. It was an incredible thing to realize that I fit in nicely as I was, as God made me. *Yep*, I thought, *very fortunate*.

Lord, I need to count my blessings from time to time,
all five feet seven-and-a-half of them.
And don't forget the half.

A Custom-Made,
Bespoke Suit

*"The heavens are the work of your hands. They will perish,
but you remain; they will all wear out like a garment....
But you remain the same."*
—Psalm 102:25–27 NIV

The other day someone asked me what *bespoke* meant. It brought back a memory.

When I arrived in New York City some twenty-five years ago, I decided I needed a new suit. An acquaintance suggested I get one custom-made—a bespoke suit. That seemed extravagant to me, but my friend was insistent. He knew a place where the cost would be no greater than at a department store and the quality and fit far superior.

I ended up at a little shop on East Sixty-second Street. After much fussing from the tailor, I chose a houndstooth pattern in Italian wool, which was then fitted to my every dimension. I remember thinking that if anything about me ever changed, I'd have to throw out the suit.

I got many good years from it, including some years at Guideposts; in fact, I wore it for my first interview with then editor-in-chief Van Varner, who said later that it made an impression. Eventually I retired it, and not long ago, during one of my periodic purges of my closet, I was faced with the prospect of actually throwing out the worn suit.

The urge to put on the suit one last time was irresistible. Would it fit? I was surprised: I'm a little broader in the chest and shoulders, narrower in the waist and hips. The pants seemed a bit too long—they must have stretched because I couldn't possibly have shrunk. Still, there was something so right about it—so *bespoke*.

Sort of like my relationship with God. In those same twenty-five years I've changed, yet God's constancy has remained unchanged. My faith has grown, but it fits me as well as it ever did.

Lord, Your love is unique for each of us.
Let me have a bespoke faith.

WINKY COAXES MILLIE ONTO CITY STREETS

"I am the LORD your God, who teaches you what is best for you, who directs you in the way you should go."
—ISAIAH 48:17 NIV

Millie and I emerged from my apartment building into the bustling Manhattan morning. After three steps, Millie crouched, dug in her paws and would go no farther, nipping at her leash. Across the street, a garbage truck noisily hoisted a dumpster into the air. Millie, my adorable ten-week-old golden retriever pup from rural Florida, cringed. She wanted no part of it. *Let's go back inside where it's safe and quiet*, her eyes pleaded.

Ten minutes of coaxing and tugging got her halfway up the block, where she promptly made a scurrying beeline back to the building, dodging the sounds of car horns, throbbing bus engines and the terrifying dumpster being slammed back to earth.

Enter Winky, who belongs to a friend of mine. Winky is a wise dog who, like most New Yorkers, is completely acclimated to the urban cacophony around us. If I couldn't teach Millie to walk around the block, maybe Winky could.

We met Winky outside my building that afternoon. I had to drag Millie across the lobby and out the door, but the instant she spotted Winky, she perked up. Winky started up the street; Millie took a few steps after her, then put on the brakes. "C'mon, girl," I said.

Winky stopped and glanced over her shoulder. By now Millie was flat on the sidewalk, her puppy paws splayed, ears back, tongue hanging out, but I could see the two dogs' eyes meet. Winky waited, then turned. Millie looked up at me as if to say, *All right, I'll try.* An instant later she was right behind Winky, her legs pumping to keep up.

Lord, I still have fearful puppy moments when this world seems overwhelming. Yet You're always there to lead me through.

⁂⁂

MOM STEALING?

"Remember the LORD in a distant land,
and think on Jerusalem."
—JEREMIAH 51:50 NIV

My mother moved into an assisted-living home after Alzheimer's made it impossible for her to live alone. She'd only been there a week when I got a call from the supervisor. "I hate to tell you this, but your mom's been swiping things from other people's rooms. Socks, candy bars,

T-shirts. Nothing big, except that one lady's cross is missing."

My mom? Stealing? This was the most honest person I knew, who once drove twenty miles back to a store where the clerk had given her too much change—less than a dollar and considerably less than it cost in gas to return the overage.

The next time I visited, I gently chided her for the pilfering. "You've got to cut that out, Mom," I said, sitting with her in the lunchroom. "Did you take that cross?"

She shook her head, her curly gray hair bouncing.

"Sure about that?" I pressed.

Mom turned away, then reached into her purse and pulled out the small silver cross. She set it down on the table gingerly and stared at it. "I wasn't trying to steal" was all the explanation she gave.

Later I turned over the cross to the supervisor, apologizing. "Don't, don't," she said. "Your mom's a charmer. She's just trying to hang on to the things that mean the most to her."

The next time I came out I brought Mom a small silver cross. She stopped stealing after that.

Eventually we had to move Mom to a facility where she could receive more care and where, of course, she charmed everyone. She even led prayers on Friday morning. She had forgotten almost everything else, yet the prayers came to her lips as if she had freshly committed them to memory. And when she died, the saddest people of all were the people she prayed with on Friday morning with that little silver cross I gave her clutched in her hand.

Lord, Mom is with You now. Teach me never to forget You,
just as You never forgot her.

##

Have a Perfect Day? Bah!

And let thy heart cheer thee.
—Ecclesiastes 11:9

I see a salesman named Mel in the locker room at my gym nearly every workday morning. He always one-ups the good-cheer brigade by exhorting me to "Have a perfect day!"

Invariably I reply, cringing inside, "If you insist."

This week, though, Mel is on vacation. Perhaps because I'm so accustomed to his hyperbolic salute, yesterday I found myself still grumbling, *Why does he always say that? Is it even possible to have a perfect day?* Naturally, we all have good and bad days, but nothing on earth is perfect, especially my typical day.

Like yesterday. I squabbled with a cashier, then upbraided her for being curt with me. I was testy with my wife on the phone and quite impatient with my dogs at their noon walk. I got off on the wrong foot on a work assignment and had to throw out everything I'd done. By four o'clock I was reaching for the aspirins and antacids and complaining to a friend on e-mail what a dismal waste the day had been. "When I feel that way," he typed back, unduly cheery, "I make a gratitude list."

Bah! I was more interested in making an ingratitude list. But almost involuntarily I found myself mentally checking off those things for which I knew I should be humble and grateful, even at the end of a horrible day: My friends were still my friends; my wife was still my wife; my health was strong; my job would still be there in the morning, my dogs—like all dogs—were the most forgiving creatures on the planet. And there was God, who loves and hears me day after day, good and bad, no matter what.

I thought again of Mel's daily greeting. I've missed it this week. When he gets back and bellows it out, as I know he must, I'll be sure to reply, "I will."

God, help me realize that like all Your gifts,
the days that You give me are perfect, even when I am not.

❋❋❋

AT PICASSO MUSEUM
IN BARCELONA

My flesh and my heart faileth:
but God is the strength of my heart, and my portion for ever.
—PSALM 73:26

I spent a fascinating afternoon a few years ago wandering the Picasso Museum in the artist's hometown of Barcelona, Spain. The Museu Picasso is found on Carrer Montcada in Barri Gòtic, the ancient heart of Barcelona, a warren of cobbled streets and medieval structures. The museum itself occupies a row of five gothic palaces, and the architecture alone is worth the visit.

Pablo Picasso wasn't actually born in Barcelona but moved there in 1894 when his father, an art teacher, found work in the city schools. Picasso was certainly precocious—he had his first exhibition at fifteen—and didn't even bother to sign his work in the beginning. The museum is full of those early pieces, room after room of them. And there is one thing that struck me about most of it: It was really bad.

No wonder he didn't sign anything, I thought to myself. Finally, after looking at some awkward paintings of the

Barcelona shoreline, I mentioned my impressions to a guard. He chuckled and said, "Well, sometimes you have to be bad before you can be good."

Picasso became more than good. He was arguably the greatest, and certainly the most influential, artist of the twentieth century, though it would be some time after his Barcelona years that he would finally sound his genius in Paris. So maybe he had to be really bad before he could be really great.

God, our paths are littered with courageous failures.
Let me always remember that oftentimes
I have to be bad before I can be good.

###

DEVOTED TO SPINNING

Incline thine ear unto wisdom,
and apply thine heart to understanding.
—PROVERBS 2:2

I am devoted to a form of aerobic insanity known as spinning, a heart-pounding, leg-pumping, sweat-drenched stationary bike workout set to loud, thumping music. I take a class a day, as many as four hundred spin hours a year. Some people jog, some people stretch, some people walk the mall. I spin.

The other night I rushed from the office and slipped into a popular spin room at my gym to stake out a good bike before I changed into my biking gear. I heard some people in the back of the spin room giggle, and I thought I heard the name Mark or Clark. I tied my towel to the handle bars of the bike I favored, dashed into the locker room to change clothes and raced back into class just as the instructor was cranking up the music. Before long I was huffing and puffing and groaning, pedaling up simulated mountain terrain, doing sprints and jumps and surges, pushing my heart rate to ninety percent of maximum.

Afterward, I stopped by the juice bar for a bottle of water. Again the giggles started. *What's up with these people?* I wondered.

Finally, a woman spoke. "Know what your nickname is?" she asked.

"I didn't know I had one," I said, fighting off embarrassment.

"You run in there in your suit and tie and glasses, then reappear a minute later and ride your bike like Superman or something. We always say, 'Look out, here comes Clark Kent!'"

All right, I had to laugh. In fact, we all had a pretty good laugh.

Maybe I am a little serious about my exercise, and I guess it shows sometimes by the way I behave. But I don't really think of myself as Clark Kent, and I know I'm no Superman. I can get carried away with my spinning, though. It's probably not a good idea to be so overwhelmingly focused on something. I'm going to remember that, thanks to my spinning friends.

Lord, let me remember where the real focus
must always remain—on You.

❈❈❈

PRAYING AT THE DOG RUN

Wondrously show Your lovingkindness,
O Savior of those who take refuge at Your right hand.
—PSALM 17:7 NASB

The dog run where I take Millie for her exercise and canine social life is also an interesting place to observe people. The other day I overheard a conversation between two women sitting next to me on a bench.

Older Woman (OW): What day is it?

Younger Woman (YW): Fifteen.

OW: Congratulations.

YW: Thanks. I never thought I'd make it, especially last night. I really wanted to.

OW: But you didn't.

YW: No. But I'm ashamed of myself for wanting to. I just kept praying and the urge passed. I went to a meeting first thing this morning and talked about it to the group.

OW: What will you do the next time the urge hits you?

YW: Pray. Pick up the phone. Find a meeting.

OW: You're going to be all right then. Don't be ashamed. The one thing you can always do is pray. God understands.

YW: I never believed in God, let alone prayer, before. Now it's saving my life, I guess.

OW: I'm praying for you too, dear. Lots of people are.

The older woman rose and retrieved her dog, and the younger woman pulled out a book. I watched Millie chase another golden retriever in a big circle until they skidded to a stop. Then I stole a peek at what the woman was reading—the Big Book, the Alcoholics Anonymous spiritual blueprint for recovery from alcoholism, a day at a time. She turned the page, and I closed my eyes. She had one more person praying for her.

You are there for us, God,
as our highest power in our hardest times.

⊕⊕⊕

FACE-TO-FACE
CONTACT FEELS GOOD

I would not write...but I trust to come unto you,
and speak face to face.
—2 JOHN 12

"E-mail's down!"

I must have heard that message three times the other morning between the elevator and my desk. Hanging up my coat, I could only sigh in resignation as I glanced at my barren computer screen. When it would be fixed was anyone's guess because, well, e-mail was down and no one could communicate. No matter. It would probably be back up by lunch.

Noon came and no e-mail. By three o'clock, the tech department's "help desk" was no longer even answering its phones. I threw up my hands and stalked down the hall to deliver a manuscript to an editor to whom I would have normally e-mailed my suggestions. I just hoped she could read my handwriting. "Oh, who's that?" I asked, noticing a snapshot of a newborn on her bulletin board.

"That's my nephew!" she said proudly, pulling out some more pictures from her desk.

"Wow, your first one?"

"Yep."

"Congratulations. By the way, nice work on this story."

"Thanks."

I walked back down the hall wondering when was the last time I'd stopped by her office. It struck me how nice it felt just to hand something to someone, have a look at a bulletin board and exchange a few words. It's become entirely too easy, I decided, for people to avoid actually talking to each other. Yes, a lot of our technology shrinks the world and makes it easier for us to communicate. But it can also make it easier for us not to communicate. And that's shrinking the world too much.

By the time I got back to my office, I hoped my computer screen was still blank. Thankfully, it was.

God, don't let me forget that people are more important than technology. Maybe that's what You're trying to tell me when the e-mail crashes.

##

BETTER CARE FOR MY BODY

Know ye not that your body is the temple of the Holy Ghost which is in you?
—1 CORINTHIANS 6:19

Perhaps because I recently had a physical, I'm thinking about my body today. I've been using it now for more than fifty years and abusing it at times too. There have been fractures and contusions, the usual assortment of minor illnesses, plus the occasional aches and pains, a minor surgery, and a couple of invasive medical procedures, a number of repaired teeth, and eyes that can no longer see things at a distance unaided.

Over the years I've subjected this body of mine to both exercise and sloth (though mostly exercise these days), a few bad habits that I pray are thankfully behind me, questionable food choices and diets, too little sleep and sometimes too much caffeine, many different time zones (jet lag shortens your life, but only by a few hours, it turns out), and stress I should have known how to avoid. Yet despite all this, I'm still breathing, walking, talking, thinking.

Maybe this is the key: God has taken better care of my body than I have. He installed me in it, after all; it makes sense that He'd keep an eye on it. And the longer I use it, the more gratitude and appreciation I have for the many incredible ways it has served me. In fact, I wouldn't mind if it lasted another fifty years or so.

Father, You created Adam from dust and gave him human form. I thank You for the gift of my physical being. I promise in the years ahead I'll take better care of it.

FALL

Now the God of hope fill you with all joy and peace
in believing, that ye may abound in hope,
through the power of the Holy Ghost.

–ROMANS 15:13

CHEERING FOR THE
WOLVERINES

The ways of man are before the eyes of the LORD.
—PROVERBS 5:21

I was at Michigan Stadium, cheering for my beloved Wolverines. My sister and I were on our annual pilgrimage to Ann Arbor for a football game. This year it was against highly ranked Notre Dame, extra incentive to cheer on my team.

The first half was tight, and as halftime arrived my voice was getting hoarse. I decided to brave the hordes and get a soda. I inched my way down the long, narrow bench with painted-on numbers that passes as a row of seats in the "Big House" and was about to squeeze into the aisle when a hand shot out and tugged at the elbow of my maize and blue sweatshirt.

"You're Edward from *Guideposts*," said a woman.

"We recognized you from your picture in the magazine," chimed in a man I presumed to be her husband.

How incredible that in a crowd of 111,000 screaming fans, this couple had picked me out. A little startling too. I normally try to be on my best behavior, but I have to admit that sometimes things slip out of my mouth at a Michigan game that ordinarily wouldn't and shouldn't.

The couple was from Ohio. They happened to be driving across the country and a pair of tickets to the game fell into their hands. "We decided it would be an exciting way to start the journey, and here we are meeting the editor of our favorite magazine," the woman explained.

We chatted for a while, and I returned to my seat where

I turned to my sister and asked, "I didn't say anything I shouldn't have during the first half, did I?"

Mary Lou laughed. "No, you were fine."

Enthusiasm is a good thing, and I have it when it comes to Michigan football. But I've also got to remember to behave myself. You never know who might be watching.

God, we're always visible to You. Let the love of Christ show forth in all my words and deeds, even in the heat of Wolverine football at the "Big House."

<hr>

THUNDER, LIGHTNING, AND WE WERE AIRBORNE

When thou passest through the waters, I will be with thee; and through the rivers, they shall not overflow thee.

—Isaiah 43:2

I was driving through a rainstorm in upstate New York one Friday, headed east on Route 23 toward my house in Great Barrington, Massachusetts. Millie, barely a year old, was curled up in the back of the Jeep in her dog bed.

There was a crack of thunder, and lightning slashed at the Berkshire Hills ahead. Then, negotiating a curve beside a nearly overflowing swamp, I felt the wheels slip from under me. Foolishly, I must have hit the brakes instead of steering with the skid. We veered off the road toward the swamp, and all of a sudden we were airborne.

The Jeep rolled once, twice, bouncing crazily down an embankment, so fast and so violently that there was no time for my mind to register it. We landed wheels down in the swamp a good twenty feet from shore and in about three feet of water. Mud and ooze caked the windshield. The passenger's side roof was crushed; water sloshed over the floorboards.

Millie! I undid my seatbelt, pushed the door open and waded to the back of the Jeep. She was trembling with fear but otherwise unharmed. I popped the hatch. "Honey, you're going to have to learn to swim," I muttered, easing her out into the water and steering her toward shore, one arm under her belly. She struggled to keep her chin above the muck and paddled heroically. "Good girl!"

Cars had pulled over and people met us with blankets and looks of amazement. One woman, a total stranger, hugged me and said, "It's a miracle you survived. I saw the whole thing. There was an angel watching over you and your dog."

I was aware of very little when the Jeep flipped over. But Someone was in control.

I have no doubt now, God, that in my greatest need
You are closer than ever.

LESSONS FROM MILLIE

Ask now the beasts, and they shall teach thee.
—Job 12:7

I'll never forget the moment I first laid eyes on Millie. Actually all I saw was her wet black nose poking out of a puppy kennel stacked on an airline luggage cart. My wife Julee and I lifted the kennel to the ground and opened the door. After some hesitation our little golden retriever emerged, looking both relieved and overwhelmed at the activity around her. *Millie*, I thought, *you have so much to learn, and I'll teach you.*

Well, wouldn't you know it, she's probably taught me as much as I've taught her. A few lessons from Millie:

- *When you're happy, let the world know.* For such a sweet, gentle dog, Millie has a monster bark. But she doesn't bark much except when she's happy. She reminds me that joy is contagious and there's no reason to keep it in.

- *Hold your tail up.* A trainer observed that Millie exhibits confidence by walking with her tail held high. "It makes other dogs feel relaxed around her." I should hold my head up when I walk down the street.

- *Play, play, play.* Learning to be a city dog is *serious* business. It takes a lot of concentration and practice. But don't forget to play like crazy whenever the opportunity presents itself.

- *Be thankful.* For every meal, every walk, every nap, every friend. With a nuzzle or a lick, Millie says "Thank you." I should remember to be grateful in all things too.

- *Stay in the now!* Millie greets each day as if it's the greatest adventure of her life. Her whole body wags at the prospect of a morning walk. For me, staying in the moment is the only way to experience God in my life. He is here now, in the moment, the greatest adventure life holds.

*Thank You, God, for Millie and all the ways
You use her to teach this old dog new lessons.*

A BIT OF ANCESTRY FOUND

Seek, and ye shall find; knock, and it shall be opened unto you.
—MATTHEW 7:7

The milky computer screen seemed out of place in the Emigration Room of the Irish National Library in Dublin. On vacation last fall in Ireland, I had dropped by the stately old Georgian building to see an exhibit on Jonathan Swift, when I spotted this little room set aside principally for Irish Americans like me who are curious about their ancestors.

My mother's father's family, the Rossiters, came over from County Wexford before the Revolutionary War. The McBrides, my mother's mother's people, were from Wicklow. My paternal grandmother's family, the Daleys, were said to be from Cork. But Grinnan? No one could figure out Grinnan.

Except now, after a few clicks of the computer mouse, here I was staring at a page from a genealogical database, looking back in time to the records of the parish of St. Sebastian in County Offaly in the mid-1840s—to a family by the name of Grinnan. There were Mary, Seamus, Liam, Thomas, Elizabeth, Patrick, living not far outside the town of Tullamore. Yet no sign of them after that. Nothing.

I was perplexed until I consulted a dusty collection of ship's manifests—famine ships, embarking from Liverpool to the U.S. There I found a few of those same Grinnans listed as passengers. Not all of them made it to Liverpool in 1845, the beginning of the Great Hunger that killed more than a million Irish and drove twice that many from their homeland. Most of the Grinnans had been wiped out by the famine, it seemed, and there was no telling who out of those who'd made it onto ships actually survived the horrific crossing. But someone had. Someone whose name I still carried. Closing the manifest, I felt a wonderful shiver of unexpected recognition.

I'd come to Ireland for the museums and bookshops, for the Abbey Theatre and Bewley's Oriental Café, for the land and the sea. But almost by accident, with a click of the computer mouse, I'd been connected to a misty past and a historic tragedy and found a piece of myself.

Family is the road You give us to travel in life,
Father, each generation another step in the journey to You.

\#

AILEEN,
MY HAIRDRESSER-FRIEND

But I have called you friends.
—JOHN 15:15

There is a woman whom I follow everywhere in New York. Her name is Aileen, and she cuts my hair. I first encountered Aileen when she worked at the salon in Bloomingdale's, and I had a half-price coupon for hairstyling. I liked what she did with my obstreperous locks—somehow she got them to behave. So when Aileen moved from Bloomingdale's to a little shop on East Fifty-eighth Street, I loyally followed. When she left that job without another to go to, she came by my apartment and cut my hair over the kitchen sink. Later, she was hired by what I was told was *the* trendiest salon in Manhattan, where patrons booked weeks in advance and paid a pretty price for the privilege. Aileen and I didn't feel comfortable there. We moved on.

Aileen was quite young when we started, and I was, well, *younger*. She lived an exuberant nightlife back then, sometimes showing up for her first appointment without having gone to bed. I saw her meet the man of her dreams, get married, and join a venerable old Dutch Reformed Church in the East Village. Her work area used to be covered by postcards from downtown art galleries and dance clubs. Now she keeps pictures of her young son and his grandmas.

We're settled in now, the two of us, at another department store salon. It's funny to think I've known Aileen longer than I've known my wife or been at my job. My hair is starting to show just a touch of gray. I've never socialized with Aileen outside of her work and I've never seen her without a pair of clippers in one hand, but yesterday while she was finishing up by disciplining my cowlick with some hair gel, she said, "You know, you've changed." I thought she was going to tell me my hairline had eroded some since my last visit, but no. "You're mellower," she said.

I don't quite know what that means, "mellower." But I've been thinking it over and the next time I see this woman—not exactly a close friend but certainly not a stranger—I have something to tell her: We've mellowed together.

I am thankful, God, not just for the people
You bring into my life but for those whom
You keep there as we journey on Your path.

Estelle Grinnan's
Never Been Sick

Fear not them which kill the body, but are not able to kill the soul.
—Matthew 10:28

When I tell people my mother suffers from Alzheimer's, they invariably ask if she still recognizes me. I am relieved to say she does, for now, though this will probably not continue to be the case. Yet the question I increasingly ask myself is: Do I recognize her?

This was a woman who continued to jog well into her seventies. Her favorite pastimes included shoveling snow and mowing the yard. She relished telling you she had never been sick a day in her life, and on the rare occasions when she admitted that a cold might be coming on, she liked to combat it by scrubbing the kitchen floor, as if hard work was the only tonic to malaise. You suspected she didn't quite understand people who got sick.

When the time came to take away her driver's license, I will never forget my brother and sister and I standing guiltily around Mom's kitchen table while she shook her head defiantly, much too stubborn and proud to cry *or* plead—after all who were we, her children, to tell her what she couldn't do? After that, she walked the three miles to church nearly every morning. She counted the money from the collection basket, though someone always quietly recounted it after Mom began slipping. For a long time she was the church librarian, though again, in later years, she had trouble reshelving the books correctly and had to be checked.

My mother will still tell you she has never been sick a day in her life. She told me that very same thing this morning, in fact, from the hospital where she had been taken when she couldn't get out of bed. She is failing physically now. The ravages of osteoporosis, a stubborn intestinal disorder, high blood pressure—these are the wolves that circle her. At eighty-five and barely able to understand what is happening and why she is in pain, Estelle Grinnan is not the person I once recognized as my mother.

But then there is that strange but nonetheless resounding declaration of health despite the tubing that invades her, the cumbersome back brace that is supposed to relieve the pressure on her crushed vertebrae, the X-rays and blood tests and CAT scans and sonograms, the whole unnerving high-tech arsenal of modern medicine. There is, after all, somewhere in all of that corporeal wreckage of a long life well-lived, a woman who has never been sick a day in her life.

Lord, at the end of our journey,
we are still the people You made us.

❈❈

LISTEN RATHER THAN REACT

He who answers before listening—
that is his folly and his shame.
—PROVERBS 18:13 NIV

Julee and I had had a fight. We hadn't exactly hung up on each other, but almost. We were each pretty itchy to end the conversation first.

We don't like being mad at each other, and we certainly don't fight like we used to when our marriage was new. Back then, we were still testing each other's limits and learning how to compromise. Some days I wasn't sure our marriage would survive. But a wise mentor to whom I eventually brought my problem helped me.

"She's too emotional," I told him, as we walked along Central Park West. "She takes everything personally."

After a few minutes of this, he said, "And what about you? A fight takes two and all you've talked about is Julee."

Well, I thought, *isn't she the problem?*

"I just defend myself," I said.

I wanted to take back those words as soon as I said them. My friend smiled and then nodded. "That's why most couples fight," he said. "Because they're too busy defending themselves and not listening. If you want to stop fighting, start listening. Here's a trick: Try repeating back to her what you thought she said. See if you both hear the same thing. You won't stop fighting until you start understanding each other."

Listen rather than react. Understand instead of defend. Lo and behold, we stopped fighting and started talking things out more. We had our blowups for sure; now we knew how to call a truce. Through the years we fought less and less. But we had to *practice* not fighting.

Maybe I'm out of practice, I thought, picking up the phone to call Julee. It would be good to hear her voice.

> *God, You brought Julee and me together for a reason,*
> *and it wasn't to fight. Help us keep our ears open*
> *so that our hearts may stay open.*

\#

SALLY BROWN
MAKES A BEELINE

Has not God chosen those who are poor
in the world to be rich in faith?
—JAMES 2:5 RSV

My little dog Sally Brown teaches me many things, and as usual I learn in spite of myself. The other day on my lunch hour I was impatiently walking her around the block (dragging might be a better word). I didn't have much time, and I let her know it. But cocker spaniels have relentless noses.

Around the corner came a man—I'm tempted to say old man, but there was really no telling—dressed in a soiled and ragged overcoat, grubby strands of dark hair half-tucked up under a frayed watch cap, his eyes sagging and sad. I, a seasoned New Yorker, glanced away.

But Sally made a kind of scurrying beeline to him, her stubby remnant of a tail vibrating in excitement. It was an utter mystery to me why she picked out this sorry soul to greet with the joy of a long-lost friend. My hand tightened on the leash. I wanted to pull her back, but self-consciousness got the better of me and I slackened my grip.

Sally sat demurely, obligingly allowing herself to be adored and stroked by the grimy hands. She gazed up at her admirer appreciatively. His features softened, a spark ignited in his eyes, and he smiled. "You *beeeaauutiful* girl, you!" he exclaimed quietly. "Thanks for saying hello."

He never looked at me. Quickly, he straightened up and was off. I stood and watched the man disappear down the street, wondering how he would have responded if it had been I who had stopped to say hello.

God, sometimes Your smallest creatures have the largest hearts.
Help me do unto others with a larger heart.

##

WORRY—A FORM OF
PRAYER AND LOVE

I will be glad and rejoice in your love, for you saw my affliction
and knew the anguish of my soul.

—PSALM 31:7 NIV

My mom was a world-class worrier. All moms worry; that's their job. But no one worried more fervently than Estelle Rossister Grinnan. If I was late coming home, she didn't just worry about where I was or what might have delayed me; she was already fretting over funeral arrangements. "I didn't know if we should bury you back in Philadelphia, where the family plot is, or out here in Detroit, where you grew up."

"Mom!"

"The Lord only knows where you've been."

"Mom, that's crazy."

"What, I'm not allowed to worry about you?"

As I got older and developed a more mature appreciation for the strength of my mother's faith, it puzzled me that a woman who believed so deeply could still worry so much. Didn't her faith protect her from such anguish? One day I asked her.

"Oh no," she said. "I believe God worries, too, about us, even with us. Jesus worried. He wept. When I worry, I feel closer to Him, like we're working on the problem together. And you know, I can't worry without praying. It's the same thing sometimes. If I couldn't worry, I'd go crazy! How can you love and not worry?"

Mom handled her worry by making it a spiritual exercise, a way to grow closer to the God she knew protected her. Worry was not just a form of prayer but a form of love.

*Dear God, if I can't be spared from
a worry or two, especially for the people I love,
please let my worries draw me closer to You.*

##

THE DAY
PRESIDENT KENNEDY DIED

*May the God who gives endurance
and encouragement give you a spirit of unity
among yourselves as you follow Christ Jesus.*

—ROMANS 15:5 NIV

On November 22, 1963, I was nine and in fourth grade at Meadow Lake School in Birmingham, Michigan. It was a raw, overcast Friday, but we were sweaty under our bulky jackets and flushed from playing at recess. We clattered back to our desks, eager to hear Mr. Schaeffer read another chapter from *Champion Dog Prince Tom*, about a wayward cocker spaniel who triumphs as a show dog.

Mr. Schaeffer stood by the intercom, his forehead resting against the speaker, as we all came in. Then he turned to us, his eyes red. Mr. Schaeffer, the brush-cut ex-Marine, had been crying.

"Your parents will explain," he said softly. "Classes are canceled. We all need to be with our families now."

Out our classroom window, I saw the yellow line of school buses filing slowly into the parking lot, early by a couple hours. By the time we had all piled onto them, there were whispers that something had happened to President Kennedy. Billy Costello said he was dead; he'd heard it on his transistor radio. No one wanted to believe him.

My dad was already home from work when I got there. He and Mom were glued to the TV, pale and shaken, and I heard Walter Cronkite say that the president had been assassinated.

The skies opened up and the rain came in torrents that night against my bedroom window. My mom sat silently on the edge of the bed in the dark for a long time while I pretended to sleep.

Mr. Schaeffer was right. We needed to be with our families, and, in a way, the country itself became a family that long gray weekend, watching the funeral procession on TV, united by grief yet sharing a strength that helps us endure even the greatest trials together.

Father, our country faces great challenges.
Help us to remember that, like a family,
we are strongest when we are united.

###

THE WHAT-IFS

When anxiety was great within me,
your consolation brought joy to my soul.
—PSALM 94:19 NIV

The call from my wife Julee came in right before 5:00 a.m. She was in the Berkshire Hills where she was getting our house ready for a Thanksgiving family gathering. I planned to take the train up from New York City on Tuesday night, but now everything had changed.

"I fell down the stairs," she moaned. "The paramedics are here. It looks like I broke my collarbone. I'm going to the hospital."

"I'll be there as fast as I can."

"Call someone to come over and take care of Millie. She's hysterical." Our young golden retriever had never seen a commotion like this. Who were these strangers and why were they taking Julee away?

I threw some things in a bag, called our friend Chrissy to check on Millie and then go over to see Julee in the emergency room, and ran the few short blocks to Penn Station where I got a seat on the next train, due to leave in an hour's time.

What a long hour it was, pacing outside the station, too distracted even to focus on a coherent prayer. *What if Julee needs surgery? What if it's worse than just a fractured clavicle?*

"The what-ifs will drive us crazy," I recalled a friend once telling me. *What if,* I suddenly reminded myself, *God is in charge, and I just need to step out of the way and calm down?*

That's the what-if that mattered. Julee did break her collarbone, but she was going to be okay, and we had an interesting Thanksgiving with me doing the cooking. Millie was her joyous self once we were all reunited. *What if,* I reminded myself again a few days later as we waved goodbye to my family, *after all these years I just learn to let God take charge when I can't?*

Father, You never fail us in times of need.
Next time I'll try to remember
the most important what-if of all.

###

TURNING FIFTY

Perfect love casteth out fear.
—1 JOHN 4:18

Well, this is how the conversation went the year I turned fifty: *I'm not sure I'm ready to be fifty.*

I was ready to turn forty. At forty, you're just hitting your stride, poised at the demographic meridian of life and finally ready to put all your learning years to good use. At thirty, I was simply relieved to have survived my twenties. At twenty...well, at twenty I didn't even think about birthday milestones (except maybe turning twenty-one). Yet here I am on the precipice of fifty, and for the first time in my life I find myself troubled by a birthday. Am I one of those foolish middle-aged men trying to hang on to youth?

Here are three things I'm trying to keep in mind as I approach fifty: First, we don't live forever. Second, life is a gift, and it should only grow more valuable as we grow older. And third, the only truly important thing in life is love.

Without love we die, at least on the inside. Nothing makes us feel better than love. When love is called for, nothing will substitute, and when we try to substitute something for love it always ends badly. Without love, we cannot know each other and we cannot know God.

In fifty years, I've received an incredible amount of love, a staggering half century of it, and I've tried to give love as best I can, often clumsily and fitfully, even foolishly, to other humans, to animals, to ideas and beliefs, to my work, my country, and to God. Love moves like the speed of light; it never ages, even when we do. So, I tell myself, *If you want to hold on to your youth, hold on to love*. Even as I near fifty, my learning years are not entirely over.

Let me be thankful, Lord, for every year You give me,
and the love that grows with it.

##

SAY A PRAYER
FOR MY BROTHER

Pray without ceasing.
—1 THESSALONIANS 5:17

My older brother was typically matter-of-fact in his manner, even if the news he had was not. "The biopsy came back. I have cancer," he told me over the phone from Detroit. On balance, he continued, there was more good news than bad. Doctors caught it early—the most important thing—and there was an encouraging prognosis with surgery and follow-up treatment. Yet there was that one dreadful word, *cancer*. Still, I did not make the mistake of telling my brother I would pray for him.

Later, though, I talked with my sister-in-law, who told me that my brother's graciousness was being sorely tested. "With all these people saying they're going to pray for him, well you can imagine!" she laughed. I laughed, too, picturing the look on his face, that skeptical scowl I knew so well.

My brother, a hard-nosed lawyer, has never put much stock in prayer or religion. Miracles he places in the same category as fairy tales. Telling him you're going to pray for him is like serving steak to a vegetarian. It doesn't go over very well. Yet, I wonder, does the person prayed for really have any say in the matter? I don't think you can be sued over praying for someone. And I don't believe that God pays any less attention to prayers said for agnostics or even atheists. Besides, praying is a two-way street. The person may not want them, but doesn't the pray-er have rights? We have no choice but to pray! After all, praying is believing.

My brother's news stunned and frightened me. I must admit, though, that I am pleased to think of all these people praying for him, the old skeptic. So if you feel like saying a prayer, say one for my brother. But don't tell him.

Dear God, watch over all Your children,
believers and nonbelievers alike.

AN ENGLISHMAN
NAMED TERRY

Thou shalt love thy neighbour as thyself.
—MARK 12:31

I look forward to sitting in the whirlpool at my gym with an Englishman named Terry, who is wheelchair-bound. I've long since stopped offering to help him out of the chair.

"It's good exercise," he explains, hoisting himself into the steamy, burbling water. Terry has always struck me as quite at ease with himself and that makes it pleasant to be with him.

One day I got around to asking what he did for a living. "I own an introduction service," he said. "My job is to bring together people who might be right for each other. They can take it from there, if I've done my job."

"You must do a lot of background checking to make sure your clients are compatible."

Terry nodded. "You would think so, but that's not the real secret." He shifted in the water so that he could look at me. "First we have to find out if they are compatible with themselves.

"You see," he continued, "until a person is comfortable with who he or she is, there's no sense trying an introduction. So many people are looking for a partner simply because they don't want to be alone. We try to find people who are content with who they are."

Terry reached for his towel and moved toward his chair. Reflexively I went to help but he held up his hand. "I'm fine," he said. Then, with a touch of pride he added,

"Sitting in an office in New York, I bring good people together from all over the world."

We are meant to find joy in our work by bringing something of ourselves to the process. Terry has a lot to bring. He wears a wedding ring, but I haven't gotten around yet to asking him how he met his wife. I do know one thing: Someone got lucky.

Father, only when I can love the person You've made me to be am I ready to love another.

\#

MOM'S BEST BIRTHDAY

Lord, thou hast been our dwelling place in all generations.
—Psalm 90:1

It was my mother's eighty-third birthday, and I was not looking forward to visiting her. She no longer could say for sure what year she was born. In the 1950s, she had been a quiz show champion. Now you couldn't even get her going anymore on baseball or politics.

On the drive to see her at the group home where my siblings and I had recently moved her, my own memory troubled me. I thought of all the times she had wanted me to visit and I hadn't come: the Easter vacation in college when I went to Key West; the Thanksgiving night I went to a movie rather than help with the dishes; the extra days I couldn't spare after my father's funeral...

I was in a bad state when I arrived at the group home, though the fierce strength of her hug was a surprise coming from the stooped figure who greeted me. "My youngest," she announced to the other residents. We sat quietly together on the screened back porch for a time when, suddenly, Mom said, "Remember my birthday when you played trombone?"

I thought she was drifting into some irritating absurdity, and then the memory fell open. I must have been about nine, and I'd just taken up the trombone. It was a sad time for Mom. We'd lost my brother in a tragic death, my older sister and other brother were off to college, and my father was away that night on business. Just the two of us were celebrating with one candle and a homely little cake.

"Until you came down the stairs playing 'Happy Birthday' on your trombone, it was the worst birthday of my life. Now I think it might have been the best."

As my mother relapsed into silence, my bad state began to turn. *God makes certain memories strong for us*, I thought, *so that when our capacity to remember begins to fail, the best can still prevail for those times we need them the most.* I felt a warm strength flow in the hug that came from my mother's frail and brittle arms. It is the strength of the spirit when the body fails, and of God bringing out the best in us.

God, help me not to dwell on my failings,
but to build on the love and goodness in my life.

MESSAGE FROM LISETTE

As cold waters to a thirsty soul, so is good news.
—PROVERBS 25:25

A chime sounded on my PC, alerting me to an interoffice e-mail just received. I found a message from someone named Lisette, addressed to every online employee in the company, announcing that she was back at work. With a flick of my mouse, I relegated the message to my electronic wastepaper basket and went back to work.

I had no idea who Lisette was. There are a good 350 people in this organization, the great majority of them situated in an exurban complex sixty miles upstate from the New York City office where I labor. We all get together every summer in an anonymous throng for the company picnic, and until recently that had been pretty much the extent of our interactions. Lately, though, like many organizations, we've forged electronic ties through e-mail, voicemail, computer faxes, and who knows what next. We are just a few simple keystrokes from becoming online buddies—a prospect, I admit, that does not naturally appeal to my somewhat solitary nature.

Oddly enough, though, as the afternoon slipped by, I found my thoughts slipping back to Lisette. Where had she been? Maternity leave? Sabbatical? Honeymoon? Illness? I had no idea what her job was, but I began feeling relieved that we had her back, flattered that she'd seen fit to let me know and a touch guilty I'd so cavalierly dismissed her message.

Later that day I picked up the phone and called my newly discovered friend and found out a little more about what she does and where she had been (it was just a brief vacation). Fittingly, her position involves corporate communications. She'd certainly done a good job with me.

Lord, let me not forget that I need to stay in touch,
not just with You but with the others You bring into my path.

##

THE "HIGHER POWER STUFF"

If ye have faith as a grain of mustard seed...
nothing shall be impossible unto you.
—MATTHEW 17:20

I hadn't heard from this old friend in years, and here she was on the phone asking for help. "I think I'm an alcoholic."

I'd heard from mutual friends that she'd battled mental and physical problems and professional setbacks. She lived in the Midwest with her husband and eleven-year-old son, but her life was falling apart and I wasn't sure why she had called me or what I could do to help.

"My husband is threatening to leave," she said, "and I'm afraid I can't be a good mom to my son."

"Have you tried AA?" I asked.

"I hate AA. I hate the folding chairs and the musty church basements. All they talk about is that higher power stuff. I don't believe in God. I'll never believe in God."

I said that from what I knew, AA wasn't a church or a religious denomination or anything like that. She could believe what she wanted to believe. "All that you have to do is want to stop drinking. Why don't you try it for thirty days? Don't drink. Go to the meetings. If it doesn't work out, well..."

"I don't believe in anything," she said quietly. "But I want to stop."

That was the end of our conversation. I had no idea if I'd done her any good or if I'd ever hear from her again.

But I did, a little less than a month later. She'd stopped drinking "for now" and started going to AA meetings "almost every day." "I just wanted you to know I'm trying," she said.

"How's it going with the 'higher power stuff'?"

There was a pause. "Well, I don't *not* believe anymore."
Then she was gone with a quick goodbye.

I held the phone in my hand for a long minute. What a
lovely word, that *not*.

*Father, we come to You on many paths and some of us can only
take the smallest steps. But I know You will be there for my friend
and all those like her. They're trying.*

❈❈

CLOUDS OF STEAM

Let brotherly love continue.
—HEBREWS 13:1

Every morning before work I like to sit in the clouds. I
mean, I sit in the men's steam room at my gym.

You hear amazing things in the clouds of steam: men's
voices bragging or complaining about work; bragging or
complaining about their wives; bragging or complaining
about their children. There's something therapeutic in sitting
in a room where you can barely see your hand in front of
your face, like sitting in white darkness and sounding off
about life.

Today there were just three of us, three dim, fleshy
outlines. Perhaps because he felt comfortably anonymous,
the man on my left suddenly said, "I haven't had a drink in
over a week."

I sat wondering what I was supposed to say to this, or if
I was supposed to say anything at all, when the man on my

right volunteered, "I haven't had a drink in five years."

"How do you do it?" the man on my left asked softly. "It's the hardest thing I've ever tried. But I know if I keep drinking I'm gonna lose everything. I saw my dad go through it, saw him lose it all. Still, I want to drink."

Then the man with five years of sobriety told an amazing story of how his life was nearly destroyed by alcohol. He talked about his recovery, the faith that he had found, and the life that he rebuilt. His voice flowed with gratitude. When he had finished, he asked the man on my left which way he was going when he left the gym. "Uptown," the man replied.

"I'll walk with you," the man said. "Maybe we'll grab a cup of coffee."

With that they were gone. Later, as I dressed in the locker room, I wondered who they were. But I couldn't tell, and it didn't matter. What did matter is that I had seen God working in a most unusual place, as is so often the case.

You never know what you'll find in the clouds.

Make me ever vigilant, God, for signs of You at work.

❋❋

BETH AND "SPINNING" HER WAY

There are varieties of working,
but it is the same God who inspires them all in every one.
—1 CORINTHIANS 12:6 RSV

On Saturday morning I teach a high-energy indoor aerobic cycling class called spinning. Most of my students are serious outdoor cyclists who are looking for some conditioning between rides. They like long, grueling simulated hill climbs—essentially running hard uphill on a bike—punctuated by vigorous sprints. I put a lot of thought into my classes, combining music and exertion to achieve the most effective and beneficial aerobic experience. I expect riders to stick to the program and climb the hill together. And, all in all, my students are pretty good at following my lead.

Except for Beth. Every Saturday she sits up front, just a few feet away from me, and invariably does her own thing: pedaling like mad when the rest of us are working slowly; sitting when we're standing and vice versa. No matter how clearly and forcefully I give instructions, she ignores them. The other morning it was so bad that I vowed to talk to her after class.

"I have about a seventy percent hearing deficit," Beth explained. "I'm usually fine, but with the music blasting and everything, it's hard for me to decipher what you're saying. So I just tune everything out and do what feels best. It's a great workout. Thank you for teaching."

I set the music a little lower these days, but half the time Beth still does her own thing. That's all right, though. Perhaps I was being a little too rigid about everyone following my routine exactly. People get what they need in different ways, and maybe I'm a better teacher since Beth taught me to lighten up a little on the bike. Yes, there are many different ways to get to the top of a hill.

Lord, help me to see that my way
is not always the only way.

LOSS AND THE PRESENCE OF GOD

For whether we live, we live unto the Lord;
and whether we die, we die unto the Lord:
whether we live therefore, or die, we are the Lord's.

—ROMANS 14:8

Recently I've dealt with the loss of several loved ones, including my mom and my dear friend Van. I include in that tearful list my beloved cocker spaniel Sally Brown, who went to her reward at age sixteen. She died in my arms on a beautiful morning when once she would have streaked through the woods out back, flaxen ears flying and tongue lolling out, chasing some enthralling scent no mere human could hope to apprehend. Those years had long since passed for Sally and, finally, I brought her to her vet's. As her life slipped away, I felt the warmth and weight of her body fully against me. The vet put a stethoscope to her chest and whispered, "She's gone."

Gone is a hard concept. Gone is a full stop. Every part of us rebels against it. When I think of my friend Van, whom I also lost, I'm tempted to think of a great emptiness where his presence once was. I knew him much better than I knew most people, and he me. To lose him was incomprehensible, as if I'd lost a part of myself.

Yet loss *is* comprehensible, but only through the presence of God in my life, who gives both life and death. To accept death, to accept loss, is to move past my pain and embrace God, trusting in His perfect love and comfort. Only He can bridge that cold gulf between loss and life, and help me forge pain into acceptance. It's only then that I can focus not on the one who died, but on the one who lived.

> *As I move closer to You, Lord,*
> *help me find Your presence that will never*
> *fade or die and is there for Mom and Van*
> *and Sally and all who have gone ahead.*

LIFE'S SMALL IRRITATIONS

Therefore let us stop passing judgment on one another.
Instead, make up your mind not to put any stumbling block
or obstacle in your brother's way.
—ROMANS 14:13 NIV

Today I have some questions:

Why don't people walk faster in the cold, so they can get someplace warm sooner?

Do folks really need to be gabbing on their cell phones at the same time they're attempting to pay for purchases, thus slowing down the line? And while I'm on the subject, if you're going to take my money, can't you at least look at me when you do?

Don't people realize that yelling, "Hold the elevator!" holds up the rest of us?

To the person who lingers over the paper in a crowded coffee shop: Can't you see there are other hungry customers waiting for your table?

And what's up with those people who don't bother filling out a deposit slip until they actually get up to the ATM?

Do fellow motorists really think that blowing the horn is going to make traffic move faster?

Finally, in a world full of God's beauty and blessings, where we see His glory and goodness at every turn, why do I allow myself to become so bogged down by life's small and unimportant irritations?

Lord, keep me from judging others. Grant me patience and understanding and the wisdom to love every moment of every day that You've given me.

TWO DIFFERENT KINDS OF ENCOURAGERS

Therefore encourage one another and build one another up.
—1 THESSALONIANS 5:11 RSV

A few years ago, when Johnny Carson's death was reported in the national media, I couldn't help noticing on *The New York Times* Web site that it was also the anniversary of the death of Winston Churchill.

No two people could have been more un-alike: One was a great national hero who seemed to have led his suffering country single-handedly through the darkest days of World War II; the other was an enigmatic entertainer from the Midwestern plains, an icon of pop culture, who was known by almost every American but not really known by anyone at all. Churchill resonated; Carson was an echo.

Yet were they so dissimilar? It can be said that Churchill changed the course of history through the sheer force of his oratory. He articulated the angst of the British people, stirred their courage, and restored their fortitude. Carson was no orator in the classical sense. Yet he, too, used language—plainspoken but with a comic edge that could be razor sharp.

I remember watching film clips of Churchill in school and being inspired. I also remember the thrilling rite of passage of being allowed to stay up late and watch Johnny. And through some of America's darkest times—Vietnam, Watergate, the oil embargo, the Iranian hostage crisis—Johnny was there, in his own way bucking us up and getting us through it and tucking us into bed. Much of history can be imagined without most people; I have trouble imagining 1940s Britain without Churchill or postwar America without Carson.

That neither man was perfect is pretty well known. Churchill was, shall we say, intemperate in his habits, and Carson was aloof—some said cold—and hard to know. Still, each was imbued with a unique presence, a gift that lifted us all.

Lord, let me be open to whomever You send to encourage me.

\#

A LITTLE GOES A LONG WAY

My mouth praises thee with joyful lips,
when I...meditate on thee.
—PSALM 63:5–6 RSV

I was gently mincing the onion on the chopping board for guacamole—gently because I didn't want to disturb

Julee, my wife. I try never to bother her during her daily quiet time.

I had made a paste of one garlic clove and two teaspoons of salt, and set it aside in a small dish. Now I added the onion to a big bowl of ripe, peeled avocados and various spices. I'm not the chef in the family, but I can follow recipe instructions.

Julee's profession as a singer can be stressful and draining, as it had been this afternoon, and she went into the bedroom for her quiet time as an antidote to the daily tumult. What puzzled me, though, was how these relatively few minutes of spiritual solitude amidst all the hours of chaos in the day seemed to make such a dramatic difference for her. Julee explained that it was a simple matter of "getting back into rhythm with God." Still, I wondered.

The guacamole was done. I dredged a finger through it for a quick taste. Something was wrong. I added a shake of hot sauce. Then a frantic dash of cilantro. Just then Julee emerged from her room, stretching.

"I ruined it," I announced. Julee smiled and pointed to the garlic and salt paste, which I'd forgotten to add. "That's not going to do it!" I snapped. My wife took the dollop of paste, whipped it through the guacamole and held out a finger full. The guacamole was transformed.

"Powerful stuff," she said. "A little goes a long way."

I dutifully thanked Julee for revealing the secret of guacamole. And of her quiet time with God.

God, a little of Your peace goes a long way.
Teach me to stay in rhythm
with You throughout the day.

GOOD MEMORIES, BLESSINGS, AND HOPE

Remember his marvellous works that he hath done.
—1 CHRONICLES 16:12

The other day I got a note from a *Guideposts* reader that was particularly poignant. Emma was a longtime subscriber who had "lived a life full of happiness and the Lord's blessings." And indeed she had: seven kids, a raft of grandkids and a great-grandchild on the way. She'd lost her husband after fifty-three years of marriage and one son in an accident, but had leaned on her faith to get through those heartbreaks. "I'm in a nursing home now and don't get out much, but don't worry about me. I'm as happy as ever and I have my memories."

How sad, I thought. *Such a rich life and now...only memories.*

Or was it so sad? I'm old enough now to have a pretty full store of memories myself. I remember my mother's giggle and my father's frown, and my late brother's goofy walk. I remember the day my family moved from Philadelphia to Detroit—the big John Ivory moving van parked in front of our house—a day charged with both sadness and the wild anticipation of an eight-year-old boy setting out for the frontier. I remember my first date (I took her to Detroit's historic Greenfield Village, where we watched a blacksmith make a horseshoe, then ate Stroh's ice cream till we were sick). I remember my first day at Yale and being dumbfounded by how old and ivied the architecture was (I learned soon enough that most of it was of fairly recent vintage made to appear older). I certainly remember the day I got my current job.

Good memories are blessings, a gift to sweeten our lives. Reading Emma's letter, I understood how fiercely I held on to mine, as fiercely as one holds on to anything precious. And as Emma knows, there's nothing sad about that.

Lord, the best memories of my life are the blessings
You've given, and they always fill me with hope.

WINTER

For thou art my hope, O Lord God:
thou art my trust from my youth.
—Psalm 71:5

FIRST DAY OF WINTER

He casteth forth his ice like morsels:
who can stand before his cold?
—PSALM 147:17

Today is the first day of winter, and in New York City the season is letting itself be known—temperature in the teens, sidewalks glazed with ice, windchill below zero.

I've always been a bit skeptical about windchill readings. Why concoct a measurement for making it even colder than it already is? I suspect this is just another way to worry us into watching the TV weather report, like the heat index in the summer. Isn't ninety-five degrees hot enough?

My wife Julee buys into this hype. If she sees me going out on a cold night without a hat or gloves, she comes chasing after me until I'm properly covered. "It's minus twenty degrees!" she'll shout, quoting the dreaded windchill factor. I'll argue, but it's no use. Suddenly I'm swathed in scarves and hats and gloves so that I can barely see. I'll grumble about how this is nothing compared to the winters I grew up with in Michigan. Usually I end up declaring, "I love the cold!" By then I'm a mummy in Polartec and breaking into a sweat.

Tonight I preemptively bundle up to walk our dog Millie, who herself is impervious to cold. In front of a church up the block, homeless men and women crowd onto a school bus. Millie and I stop. Someone says, "It's a good thing the city was ready for this. They get all the homeless off the streets when the windchill hits zero."

All right, so I was wrong—again. There is a reason for that scary number, at least for the homeless in New York City. I walk Millie back toward our apartment, feeling the sharp wind on my face but warm inside—a good way to celebrate the first day of winter.

Lord, thank You for windchill factors, heat indexes,
nagging spouses, churches that help the homeless,
and all the other ways You protect us.

##

THE SAINT OF
HOPEFUL CAUSES

But ye, beloved, building up yourselves on your most holy faith,
praying in the Holy Ghost, keep yourselves in the love of God.
—JUDE 1:20–21

One morning I woke up and there he was: St. Jude himself, sitting on my dresser, compliments of my mom, no doubt, who'd probably smuggled him in while I was asleep.

I was a teenager and not an easy kid to live with, especially for my mom, who spent most of her time worrying about me. So it was no wonder Mom, an old-school Catholic, turned to Jude, the patron saint of hopeless causes.

I rubbed the sleep from my eyes and glared at the nine-inch-tall statue. *Hopeless cause, huh?* I grabbed St. Jude, marched him out into the hallway and put him on a shelf where he wouldn't bother anybody.

That night he was back on my dresser. This time I put him up on the highest shelf, so my mother would need a stepladder to retrieve him. Mom was undeterred; Jude returned to my dresser.

I knew better than to keep fighting this battle. So there Jude stayed, quietly watching over me until I moved on to college and finally started acting like an adult and a good son.

I hadn't thought about that statue in years until the other day, when I ducked into a neighborhood church and overheard the sermon. "Today," the priest said, "we celebrate the feast of St. Jude, often called the saint of hopeless causes. Yet I believe Jude is the saint of *hopeful* causes, because all who come to the Lord in prayer believe that even the most difficult problems can be made right by God."

All these years later and I finally understood my mother. There were no hopeless causes, not even me at my teenage worst. There was only prayer and God and the infinite power of hope.

Lord, if You run into Mom up there, tell her thanks.

MOM AND THE TWELVE DAYS OF CHRISTMAS

The light shineth in darkness;
and the darkness comprehended it not.

—JOHN 1:5

One Christmas we reluctantly decided that it had become too hard on my mother to transport her from her Alzheimer's unit to Christmas dinner with the family. Osteoporosis and heart problems had set in, and she was growing increasingly feeble.

December 25 was very bright and very cold, the way it should be in Michigan. My brother Joe, my sister Mary Lou and I, along with my teenage nieces Clare and Rachel, my cousin Carol, and my wife Julee, bundled up and piled into our cars and headed to Clausen Manor to see Mom. "Does she even know it's Christmas?" I asked Julee on the way.

Clare and Rachel brought chocolates. Julee and I had a plant, which I knew Mom would water to death before the new year. Carol brought an elaborate "Twelve Days of Christmas" pop-up book. It was this last gift that captured Mom's flickering attention as she sat silently in her wheelchair. We were all chatting, when, out of nowhere, Mom began to read out loud: "On the...first...day of...Christmas, my true love gave...to me...."

We stared at her in astonishment. Mom had long since lost the ability to read. Yet she forged on, "On the...second day of..."

She stumbled and struggled. Turtledoves changed into turtle dolls, hens into hills, maids into moms. By the tenth day, she was clearly weary. I started to help her with a passage when she suddenly shot me a look I hadn't seen for quite some time and snapped, "Are you going to let me do it myself?"

An instant of stunned silence gave way to laughter, save for Mom, who cast us a strangely knowing look. Then she let the book close, apparently having forgotten she'd been reading it.

Did Mom know it was Christmas? For that one bright shining moment, we all knew it.

Lord, You brought eternal light into the world. As our bodies grow, old and feeble, give our souls strength, burning with that light.

"What's the Hurry?"

It is not good to have zeal without knowledge,
nor to be hasty and miss the way.
—Proverbs 19:2 NIV

Remember the character Arte Johnson played on *Rowan and Martin's Laugh-In* who shuffled along taking half steps, barely making any progress? Well, that's how my sixteen-year-old cocker spaniel Sally walks these days, which is hard for me because I'm usually going a mile a minute, especially first thing in the morning.

"Come on, Sal," I'll say brightly, gently tugging the leash. But underneath my happy voice I'm thinking about all the things I have to do that day, places I have to be, people I have to talk to, e-mails to be sent and answered, deadlines, obligations.

Yet Sally is oblivious, sniffing every object of interest, laboriously greeting friends and strangers alike and sometimes just standing in place, taking it all in.

"Sally!" I'll say a little more emphatically, yet still in that happy voice.

Sally will look right at me, not exactly defiant, but firm, her gaze steady despite the cataracts, her mouth set with determination. I know what she's thinking: *What's the hurry?*

Easy for her to say. What's she got to do? She's retired. When she's not eating, she's either getting ready for a nap or waking up from one. All in all, she's got it pretty easy. *Life is good. So why not take your time?*

Maybe Sally has a point. Life is good, all in all. I'm passionate about my work. I love my friends and they love me, I like to think. My wife's back is still a problem, but she told me the other day it's getting better, slowly but surely.

And then there's Sally, standing there on West Thirtieth Street just staring up at me, not all that much different from when she was a puppy not much bigger than my hand, standing at practically the same spot, looking up at me and challenging me with that same question: *What's the hurry?*

Lord, I'm so blessed by everything and everyone You put in my life. Teach me to slow down and enjoy them.

###

SINGING TO GOD

And Miriam answered them, Sing ye to the LORD, *for he hath triumphed gloriously.*

—EXODUS 15:21

Oh no, here she goes again.

I was the twelve-year-old boy standing next to my mother in the pew on Sunday morning. Mom loved to sing in church. Fortunately, it was the only time she sang, because my mother couldn't carry a tune to save her life. Yet sing she did, as if there were no tomorrow. Whatever the diametric opposite of perfect pitch is, she had it, the uncanny ability not to go anywhere near the right note.

It was bad enough going to church with your parents (I always tried to go to a different service, so I could sit with my friends), but to have that kind of attention drawn to yourself was utterly mortifying. And people did cast slightly alarmed looks in our direction, to be sure. Even when I decided to attend the "guitar service" (it was the sixties, after all), my mother followed, eager to learn a new sort of music to mangle.

I was an altar boy, and I remember serving Mass with Father Walling when my mother would launch into song. He'd wince ever so slightly, and I would imagine that he could barely restrain his hands from flying up to cover his patient, suffering ears. Instead, he would quickly summon me with the cruets of wine and water.

All protests from my siblings and me fell on (tone) deaf ears. "You are supposed to be singing, not listening," she'd say, completely unsympathetic. "Besides, I'm sure God doesn't mind my voice one bit." I envisaged God frantically putting in cosmic earplugs.

Well, today it pleases me to no end that my mother really didn't give a hoot about what anyone thought of her singing. She was singing to God, not to us, and she believed that whatever came out of her mouth came out of her soul, and it was music to His ears.

My praise, Lord, is never on pitch until it reaches You.

A Simple Cup from George

Man goeth forth unto his work and to his labour until the evening.
—Psalm 104:23

Resisting the tide of upscale espresso bars offering lattes, au laits, cappuccinos, mochaccinos, frappes, and every other exotic hybrid of coffee concoction, I still prefer to wake up with a simple cup from George, an old Korean gentleman who runs a rickety little newsstand on my block. He serves it blistering hot in a short Styrofoam container with lots of milk. George's coffee is not very good, frankly. But that's not why I go there.

George is aware that I am a Detroit Tigers fan, so during baseball season he familiarizes himself with the baseball scores on the morning sports page, so he can commiserate or congratulate me. He persists in calling me "Merit" after the brand of cigarette I used to smoke when I smoked. After all these years he still says, "You Tiger team did good last night, Merit!" Of course, George is not his real given name either, but we've grown quite comfortable with how we address each other.

It must have been fairly obvious the other morning that I'd had a rough night. I'd lain awake, tossing and turning, wrestling with my worries as I am wont to do. I mumbled for George to give me a large coffee, black. George shot me a look as he searched for a big cup. He said something I didn't quite catch through his accent: "Good worka night." I repeated my request. This time George laid a hand on my arm. "God work overnight."

"God works the overnight?" I guessed after a second.

"Yes!" George said. "God work the overnight. He take care of you worries, so you can sleep."

I suppose I could get used to those specialty coffee shops that dot my way to work in the morning, but I think I'll stick with George's watery brew to wake me up. He gives me something I can't buy...a little familiar conversation, a caring word, and an occasional bit of spiritual advice that helps me get to sleep at night.

I'll try to remember, Lord, what George says:
that You are there to carry my burdens when I need to rest.

##

CHRISTMAS FRENZY
IN NEW YORK

Let this mind be in you, which was also in Christ Jesus:
Who, being in the form of God, thought it not robbery
to be equal with God: But made himself of no reputation,
and took upon him the form of a servant.

—PHILIPPIANS 2:5–7

The first glimpses of Christmas in New York City bring me great angst. Lights and wreaths and ribbons start sneaking out well before Thanksgiving and the heralded arrival of Santa, courtesy of Macy's. *I can't believe the year is ending already!* I fret. *Think of all the things I didn't get done!* Then there are the gifts I must find, the people I must see, the plane reservations and time off work and money to pay for it all. The mental list overflows with obligations and worries. I find myself turning away from that initial splash of red and green and wishing it was still the red, white, and blue of July Fourth, when the year still held such promise!

But I have an antidote. It's a memory from a December day the year after I graduated from college. In the grip of wanderlust, I had gone south, through the Caribbean to Central and South America. I was picking my way through a bustling little marketplace high in the Ecuadorian Andes, at the far edge of the northern hemisphere. Natives had traveled many rugged miles to display their wares on blankets and in makeshift stalls, as they had been doing for centuries. Beneath a tree at the edge of the market, I saw what looked to be an old baby doll resting in a pile of straw and cloth, almost as if a child had abandoned her toy. When I looked closer, I noticed a crude wooden cross stuck in the dirt and a plain box, which my companion explained was for donations for the needy.

No blinking lights, no jolly St. Nicks, no midnight madness sales. Not even the figures of Mary and Joseph or the wise men. Just the Christ Child and the simple message that He was among us.

I didn't know at the time how persistent a memory it would become, that simplest of Nativity scenes in the Andean marketplace. But today, when the frenzy of this season gets to me here in New York, I think back to it and consider what it said to me.

Lord, You came among us in humbleness so that we would be humbled. In the celebration of Your birth, I will not forget that.

\#

HOME

God is not ashamed to be called their God:
for he hath prepared for them a city.
—HEBREWS 11:16

I look out my office window to the north and see the silvery Art Deco spire of the Chrysler Building rising above the East Side of Manhattan. To the west, I see the Empire State Building, so close I have to lean way back in my chair to view its celebrated pinnacle, the other side of which I can admire from the sidewalk in front of my apartment in Chelsea, on the West Side of town. These two skyscrapers remind me a little of church steeples, even though the huge buildings, full of law firms and advertising agencies and high-powered marketing companies, aren't remotely sacred in the traditional sense.

When I go home to Franklin, Michigan, to visit, I love to see the simple white church steeple on the Franklin Green pop into view above the trees. When I come home to New York, the Chrysler Building greets me from a distance before the highway sweeps me under the East River and up into the streets of Manhattan. If I'm coming from the west, I see the Empire State Building miles before I see anything else.

Strange how things made of concrete and glass can make my heart beat faster. Yet they do, every time. Which is why I know that I truly love this city in the deepest part of me, where things of earth can become something close to sacred. It is the holiness of familiarity, of God's presence in the enduring particulars of our lives. It is home.

Father, You create for all of us a place in this world that we love, and through that love we grow closer to You.

****

CHRISTMAS "LIGHT"
AT THE OFFICE

He...was sent to bear witness of that Light.
—JOHN 1:8

I am sitting in my office at *Guideposts* magazine on a blinding winter morning the week before Christmas—not a week when much work gets done. The sunshine bouncing off the huge building across the street makes it hard to look out the window. All is brightness and light.

Down the hall somewhere I can hear voices, mostly members of the editorial support staff. They are engaged in the good-natured holiday brawl they call Kriss Kringle, where everyone gives a gift to the person whose name they have drawn. I feel a little neglected, but grumpy editors are not traditionally included in the ceremony. With a flicker of annoyance, I start to close my door, then leave it open.

I hear Nilda squeal, followed by roaring laughter. I wonder what she got? Dana snorts and says, "I'll get you for this!" I hear the hiss of a jug of pop being opened and more wrapping paper being clawed. Amy got something good, because she sounds authentically pleased. Then again, she's always polite, and this is her first Kriss Kringle. Hope scurries past my door, the bells on her Christmas bracelet jingling, Celeste trailing her with a hastily wrapped package. Stephen says, "You're too late!" and Celia tells him to be quiet. Alan guffaws. Everyone *oohhs and aahhs* as Surujnie opens her present from Colleen. Everyone howls when Stephen opens his.

I'm glad I didn't close my door. This is a nice place to work. Especially the week before Christmas. When not a lot of work gets done. And everything is Light.

Father, You prepare me for the coming of Your Son.
Make me worthy.

###

THE JOY OF DOGS

Ask now the beasts, and they shall teach thee.
—JOB 12:7

I've had dogs all my life: my obstreperous boyhood beagle Sparky, Pete the high-strung poodle, my laid-back spaniel Rudy, the high-energy, athletic Lab Marty, cocker Sally, a true princess, and Millie, our lovable golden retriever. Yet despite their markedly different personalities, they all had one common trait: the exuberant display of happiness. (Marty used to wag his tail so hard he'd occasionally fall over.)

Maybe you have just come through the front door after being gone for all of, say, oh, thirty-seven minutes. Or you pick up your canine companion's favorite toy and wonder aloud if it's a nice day to go outside. The mere mention of food will sometimes do it. Or perhaps you've been away for a long time, and when you get home you're treated like the prodigal son. You know the dog has done nothing but fret about you, and now that you're back all those worries are unleashed in a fit of delirium. And when his exertions are finally concluded, he'll just sit there and stare at you in utter relief.

Don't assume a dog is embarrassed by these outbursts, that he might be thinking, *Look at what a fool I'm making of myself!* or *Aren't I too old to act like this?* It doesn't cross his mind. A friend once remarked that she wished she could train her dog to stay put when she came through the door. Why would anyone want to train a dog to do that? It would be like training a flower not to bloom.

God, let me never forget to praise You,
to raise my voice in joy,
to give thanks for all Your blessings
and to wag my tail like crazy when the Spirit moves me!

****

"God Loves You"

O Jerusalem, that bringest good tidings,
lift up thy voice with strength; lift it up, be not afraid;
say unto the cities of Judah, Behold your God!
—Isaiah 40:9

Most mornings I log on to my computer at work, open the e-mail program and just start hitting the delete button. Hot stock tips, instant loans, online degrees, "genuine faux" watches, rapid weight-loss programs, cyber casinos—all kinds of junk e-mail clutter up my in-box.

I rarely open up any of this junk. That's because I've gotten pretty good at identifying them by the subject line. Some of them are pure gibberish: "President's Marsupial Plan" or "Bulk Rag Injection." Some are a little more insidious: "Security Notification" or "Order Delivery Status." Some border on the sinister: "Your credit has been accessed!" But I usually see through their tricks and unmercifully delete them.

The other day an e-mail from an unknown source popped up on my screen with the subject line "God Loves You."

"Yeah, right," I muttered. "I wonder what God loves so much that He wants to sell it to me." I hit delete with a mixture of annoyance and satisfaction.

A day later it was back. I deleted it again. This time I felt a little uncomfortable; I don't like deleting God. *That's what they're counting on*, I thought. *They probably wanted to refinance my mortgage if I would kindly hand over my Social Security and bank account numbers. I didn't just fall off the turnip truck, you know.*

A couple of days passed and there it was again: "God Loves You." I hesitated, finger poised above the delete key. *I'm going to regret this*, I thought, certain I was being suckered. I opened it.

Nothing—just a blank white screen. No pitch. No product.

God loves me.

The Internet is an interesting place, and I'm not sure I could even tell you *where* it exists. But one thing is sure: Certain messages always get through.

Thank You, Lord, for the reminder that
Your love is everywhere, even in my in-box.

New Year's Resolution

In every thing give thanks:
for this is the will of God in Christ Jesus concerning you.
—1 Thessalonians 5:18

I've never been one for making New Year's resolutions. They always seem about as lasting—in my case, at least—as a Christmas tree. But this year I vowed to try to stick to one that I thought was important: Every day I would thank God for one specific thing in my life for which I was grateful.

At first it was easy. I was thankful for my family, my friends, my work, my new house in the hills, my wonderful dogs. I could thank Him for a beautiful day or even a good night's sleep. I was rolling along quite nicely with my resolution when I hit a wall—the gratitude wall.

I don't know if it was the prolonged dreariness of winter or just that I was running out of ideas, but by February I found myself floundering and unable to come up with something to be thankful for. Then my friend Charlie came to visit me one wet, miserable day. Charlie is a good deal older than I am, retired, and in pretty good health except for the arthritis that gnarls his fingers and stiffens his gait, especially on cold days.

He came into my office all bundled up and took a seat on the couch. *Ffrrip, frrip*. Off came his rubbers. *Ffrrip* went the chinstrap to his hat. *Ffrrip frrip*, and Charlie was out of his mackinaw. He smiled broadly at me. "Thank God for Velcro!" he declared.

Thank God for Velcro? I hadn't thought of that! Yet here was Charlie, for whom something as absolutely commonplace as Velcro made his struggle with arthritis so much easier. Charlie knew how to be grateful. He saw in even the smallest details of his daily life the greatest reasons to praise God. That's what I'd have to learn to do—starting right now:

*Thank You, Lord, for Charlie, who opened my eyes
to the little miracles of life You provide...especially Velcro.*

##

JUST LIKE MOM

*For this reason I bow my knees before the Father, from whom
every family in heaven and on earth is named.*
—EPHESIANS 3:14–15 RSV

Recently, when I was visiting my sister in Michigan, I noticed her clipping hockey articles from the Detroit sports pages to send to my nephew Justin, who had just started art school in Chicago.

"Ah," I said with a chuckle, "upholding a fine old family practice, are you?"

Mary Lou looked at me quizzically. I was surprised she didn't get my reference.

"When I went away to college," I explained, "Mom used to send me every single article from the local papers about the Tigers. It became kind of a dormitory joke, in fact, because there was always a huge stack of baseball clippings in my room. But I would have been even more homesick without them."

My sister laughed. "I never knew that! I guess I'm more like her than I realize."

Funny how these things develop, even subconsciously. My wife Julee says I laugh just like my mom. At night, I always get out of bed to double-check that the front door is locked, a ritual of my father's that always annoyed me. So did his jiggling of change in his pocket, yet I catch myself doing the same thing. My brother and I both insist on sitting on the aisle in church or at the movies, a habit we cultivated separately.

I watched Mary Lou write out Justin's address on a roomy manila envelope, her hasty scrawl (nearly identical to Mom's handwriting) that says, "I have so much to get done." I was satisfied to think how much my family has given me to take through life, even the little things, especially the little things: a gesture, a mannerism, a figure of speech, something that says who I am and where I came from. Next time I catch myself laughing and jiggling the change in my pocket, I'll keep in mind where I learned it.

Father, where would I be without the family You've given me?

Being Sick and Letting Go

Submit yourselves therefore to God.
—James 4:7

I haven't missed a day of work in three years...until today. I'm laid up in my apartment, fighting off a fever. Nothing serious, but my coworkers insisted I stay home. I can't blame them for not wanting to catch what I have.

Usually, when I feel something coming on, I work a little harder or push myself a little further, as if I could outrun it. I get this from my mother, who thought the best thing to do if you were getting sick was to scrub the kitchen floor or shovel snow off the driveway. Today we'd call it denial, no doubt. Personally, I see nothing wrong with a healthy dose of denial occasionally. There is, after all, a fine line between denial and positive thinking.

This time, though, there is no denying it. I am sick. Chills, fever, body aches. My wife Julee's at rehearsal all day, but she rented me a stack of videos, got the daily papers and put some soup on the stove. She went out the door, admonishing me, "Now relax and let yourself get better."

Relax? How can I relax if I just sit here and do nothing? I have responsibilities at work. I'm missing a meeting. I was supposed to call so-and-so first thing this morning. Everyone is counting on me....

Outside I hear the scrape of metal on pavement. My super Ricardo is clearing some light overnight snow from the sidewalk. A couple of taxi horns beep impatiently. A dog leashed to a parking meter woofs at a policeman writing a ticket. Overhead a jet plane follows the Hudson River north on its flight pattern into LaGuardia Airport.

Funny how the world seems to be getting along without me. Is everyone really counting on me so heavily? Or do I mistake self-centeredness for responsibility, ego for conscience?

The rest of the day I pass reading and watching movies and...relaxing. I have discovered that the biggest part of getting better is letting go and being sick.

What a challenge it is, Lord, for me to let You take over.

\#

JANUARY MORNINGS

His compassions fail not. They are new every morning:
great is thy faithfulness.
—LAMENTATIONS 3:22–23

New York City is a Christmas-tree graveyard on these January mornings, the curbsides lined with discarded Scotch and Norway pines, some still trailing bits of tinsel and the occasional ornament, waiting for collection. For our dog Millie on our predawn walks, it's an olfactory paradise. She treads carefully down the salted sidewalks with me in tow and sniffs the brown branches, requiring an occasional tug on the leash as a reminder that we can't spend all day out here.

It's strangely peaceful, this sidewalk forest, dreamlike and soul-soothing. The snow drifts muffle the city's sounds in a soft silence. People move slowly, hunched against the chill. It is the calm after the storm, I suppose. The end of the year comes in such a frantic rush—we're trying to get done everything we wanted to get done, see our families, celebrate the holidays. Who isn't exhausted by the time New Year's rolls up on us?

Yet these early days of January feel slow and purposeful, an opportunity to reconnect with God. The sun is coming up just a tiny bit earlier, but you wouldn't notice unless you are like Millie and me, out at dawn every day.

Millie veers toward another tree lying on its side. I let her inspect it briefly and then give her a little pull. It's time to move on.

Father, let me begin my new year connected to You.

<hr>

MY NEIGHBOR CHARLES

Never flag in zeal, be aglow with the Spirit.
—ROMANS 12:11 RSV

It was another hectic morning of another hectic day, and as the year drew to a close, I felt wrung out and uncertain about the future. Another birthday was about to happen and the holidays were around the corner, but I didn't feel much in the spirit of things. As I left my apartment for work, I saw my neighbor, a young man I'll call Charles, waiting in the hallway for the elevator.

Charles is dying of AIDS. He is literally skin and bones. He's in his early thirties but walks with a cane. His friends tell me that Charles' doctors want him in the hospital, but Charles postpones what he knows is inevitable. There is something gloriously tenacious and stubborn about Charles.

When the elevator came, I held the door open as Charles doddered in. We both studied a notice taped on the elevator wall: "Stunning Fire Island beachhouse for summer rent. Sign up now. Have something to look forward to and get you through the winter!" I glanced at Charles and felt uncomfortable. He would not be seeing another summer. But then I saw him brighten and tear off one of the phone numbers.

Outside, I helped Charles button up his overcoat and hailed him a cab. I opened the door as he eased himself in. I could tell he was in pain. But he managed a smile and a jaunty tip of his hat. "Thank you," he said.

Then he was off. And so was I, past the newsstand where people lined up for lottery tickets, past St. John's Hall where the homeless filed in for breakfast. I was feeling just a little bit like Charles. Stubborn and tenacious and a bit more certain.

Make me see, Lord, how much You give me to look forward to, to help get me through the winters of my life.

SHARING SILENCE

Incline your ear, and come unto me: hear, and your soul shall live.
—ISAIAH 55:3

My wife is a singer. A couple of years ago she was preparing for a concert at Radio City Music Hall when she lost her voice. Her throat doctor diagnosed swollen vocal cords due to over-rehearsing and prescribed total vocal rest. "Don't speak a word," he said. "Not a sound until the morning of the show."

Julee, I can tell you, is not the silent type, and those few difficult days were an odyssey. Everywhere she went, Julee carried a pad and pencil. Our apartment was festooned with those little yellow stick-on notes. And when it came to our having a simple difference of opinion, I would have my say, then wait for Julee to write out her response. That lull in the action invariably gave my hackles time to go down a bit. Julee's words, tempered in the very writing and devoid of vocal inflection and volume, seemed so much less threatening. I had to focus on what she wrote if I were to understand her. The funny thing was the less Julee said, the harder I had to listen. We learned a lot about communication—the importance of a passing touch, a lingering look, the communing comfort of shared silence.

Julee's voice returned stronger than ever, and the concert was a success. While she chatted with friends in her dressing room afterward, I slipped across the street and got her a small box of fudge, chocolate having been at the top of the disheartening list of foods forbidden by the voice doctor. As I put the box in her hand, she was about to say something. Then she grabbed her pad and scribbled, "Thank you!"

Thank You, God, for showing me how to listen.
In Your words I find all wisdom.

\#

A PRAYING MAN

Continue in prayer, and watch in the same with thanksgiving.
—COLOSSIANS 4:2

One year I went to the National Prayer Breakfast in Washington, DC. It was the fiftieth such annual gathering of our nation's spiritual and political leaders, and the first since the terrible events of September 11, 2001.

As is customary, the president was scheduled to attend

and lead us in prayer. Security, tight in the best of times, was unprecedented. We lined up at 6:00 a.m. to pass through metal detectors and ID checkpoints before we were permitted to enter the grand ballroom of the Washington Hilton, one of the few venues large enough to accommodate the thousands of people from around the world who were invited. I took my seat at our table and couldn't help noticing the no-nonsense men and women with their telltale earpieces ringing the upper level of the ballroom. Somewhere up there, I'd heard, there was even a sharpshooter standing by in case of the unthinkable.

The dais was crowded with luminaries, including President Bush and the First Lady. Chief of Naval Operations Admiral Vern Clark rose to speak before the president. "Most people know that I'm a praying man," the admiral said. "I'll get an urgent call sometimes asking me to join in prayer with someone in crisis." Then he noted that he couldn't remember ever getting a call in the middle of the night asking him to join in a prayer of unbounded gratitude. There was a ripple of knowing laughter among the attendees.

The world has changed after the horrors of September 11. Few of us will ever be quite the same. Yet sitting on the train back to New York after the prayer breakfast, watching the scenes of everyday life sweep past the window—schoolyards, factories, neighborhoods, shopping malls, busy highways— the admiral's comment kept clicking away in my mind, and I found myself wishing I knew his phone number.

God, let me remember not just to come to You when the moment is dark, but to bow my head always in gratitude for Your goodness and Your blessings, which are boundless in both good times and bad.

WHEN SALLY WORRIES

When anxiety was great within me,
your consolation brought joy to my soul.
—Psalm 94:19 NIV

One thing that breaks my heart is to see Sally, my
fifteen-year-old cocker spaniel, worry. I've begged
God to tell me what goes through her head when she paces
or whines or simply taps me on my leg with her paw and
gives me a plaintive look that isn't about food.

Sometimes I can figure it out. When Marty, our
yellow Lab, was staying overnight at the vet's, I knew Sally's
whimpering was her worry about him. When he was
young and used to swim way off into the lake in pursuit of
something Daddy had thrown much too far, she would pace
up and down, squinting out over the water and yelping, and
occasionally giving me a dirty look for being so reckless.
And when my wife Julee leaves town on a concert tour,
Sally will spend the first several nights sleeping pressed up
against the front door.

The worst, though, is when she worries about me. If
I'm late coming home, she'll go to Julee and nudge her, as if
to say, "Where is he? Do something!" A treat helps distract
her, but soon she's pacing and crying a little. Finally she'll
get up on her hind legs and stand vigil at the window, sore
hips and all, watching for my car in the driveway.

One time I was pulled over on the Taconic Parkway
for speeding. I promised to slow down and explained to the
trooper that I was driving a little too fast because I didn't
want my cocker spaniel to worry about me. I admit that it's

a pretty poor excuse for breaking the law, but it was the only time I ever got out of a speeding ticket.

Lord, I don't always know what my dog is thinking, but You do. Please comfort her and let her know that I'm on my way.

****

BE YOURSELF!

Do ye look on things after the outward appearance? If any man trust to himself that he is Christ's...that, as he is Christ's, even so are we Christ's.
—2 CORINTHIANS 10:7

Some years ago I was given the job of editor-in-chief of *Guideposts* after working at the magazine for a dozen years. I was a little apprehensive, not so much about the work as about being the public face of such a beloved publication.

I decided to introduce myself to the readers in an editor's column, a more-or-less standard practice for which I needed a current photograph. After sifting through my recent snapshots, our photo editor decided we needed to have professional photographs taken. "All right, you know best," I agreed, though secretly I wanted to use a shot of me hiking the Appalachian Trail with my dogs, wind-blown hair, two-day stubble and all.

I got my hair trimmed and wore my best suit. The photographer shot what must have been several thousand rolls of film. A few days later, I picked out what I thought was the best shot.

Responses to my column were warm, for the most part. A few worried folks wrote in that I looked a little young to be in charge of such a big magazine, and one suggested I find someone with some experience to help me.

Then I got the most surprising letter of all. "I was a neighbor of your sister's," the correspondent wrote, "when she and Ken and the boys lived in Columbus. I've seen many pictures of you. I remember when you graduated from college. I saw pictures from your wedding and your mom's eightieth birthday party. Don't take this the wrong way. Your picture in the magazine is nice—very official looking—but I have to say I prefer you in all those family shots I've seen through the years, where you looked natural and relaxed. That's the Ed Grinnan I know. Just remember, be yourself. Good luck!"

It was too late to do anything about the picture, but there was plenty of time to get used to my new job by just being myself. And next time, maybe I'll use the shot with the dogs after all.

You make me who I am, Lord.
Help me to be true to You by being true to myself.

****

INSPIRATION FROM THE OBITS

The LORD...is thy life, and the length of thy days.
—DEUTERONOMY 30:20

My friends sometimes accuse me of being morbid because I make a point of reading the obituary page of the newspaper. I try to read a couple of daily papers, but even on days when I'm pressed for time, I read the obits no matter what.

It helps that my local paper, *The New York Times*, has perhaps the finest obituary page in the world. You will learn about some of the most fascinating people by turning to it, people you might never have known about otherwise. One of my favorites was an Englishwoman named Megan Boyd, who tied beautiful fishing flies with the workmanship of a fine jeweler. Her fame among fishermen was unsurpassed, yet she never charged more than a dollar for her masterpieces and never in her life went fishing. Prince Charles was a regular customer, and once, when the queen summoned her to Buckingham Palace to receive an award, she declined because she had no one to care for her dog that day. The queen said she understood completely.

Obviously there are *Times* obituaries for the famous—Tom Dooley, Winston Churchill, Jackie Kennedy, Mother Teresa, even the racehorse Secretariat—and the semifamous: writers I'd never have read, musicians whose work I'd never have listened to, athletes whose accomplishments I'd have forgotten, scientists and philosophers whose ideas I'd never have known about without the help of the obituary page. But the obituaries I most appreciate are the inspiring stories of ordinary people overcoming incredible hardships or turning their lives around after disastrous personal or professional misfortune. Day in and day out, reading the obituary page makes me feel better about the world and the people in it.

"Why do you want to know who died?" friends will ask. I tell them that's not the point. I'm finding out who lived.

God, Giver of life,
let me give back to You by the way I live.

THE WESTMINSTER DOG SHOW

All who are with me send greetings to you.
Greet those who love us in the faith. Grace be with you all.
—TITUS 3:15 RSV

If you live in New York City, you're likely to bump into a celebrity sooner or later—a supermodel at the supermarket, for instance, or a movie star at the movies. Once, a starting pitcher for the New York Mets climbed out of the cab I was getting into. That was a big thrill. But my favorite celebrities are the ones I run into every year without fail.

My apartment is near the Penta Hotel, where many of the dogs competing in the legendary Westminster Dog Show at Madison Square Garden and their owners stay. I pass by the hotel early every morning on my way to the gym when these stellar champions are taking their morning constitutionals. There are greyhounds with sweaters and Weimaraners in raincoats. Some of the dogs have swanky collars and leads, and even entourages. Each and every one is a magnificent physical example of its breed.

Unlike human celebrities, though, these stars are quite approachable, and I always stop and make a fool of myself over them and ask to shake their paws. One year I got to wish the Clumber spaniel who went on to win Best in Show good luck, and it was fun watching him crowned that night on TV. (I jumped up and down shouting, "I know that dog!") The owners are pretty friendly too. Like all dog owners, they love to talk about their animals, and I have had some wonderful conversations with people from all over the country, people who are as interesting as their dogs, and usually just as friendly.

That's probably the best thing about our pets (and even dog show stars are pets). They make us friendlier people, and maybe even a bit kinder and more open. I've noticed that when we treat our pets like stars, we tend to treat one another a little nicer too.

Lord, I'm not entirely sure why You made us so crazy about our pets, but I am grateful. Maybe it was just to help us learn to be a little more friendly.

❈❈

WE ARE HERE TO HELP

Encourage the timid, help the weak, be patient with everyone.
—1 THESSALONIANS 5:14 NIV

I had a retarded brother who was four years older and idolized me. One afternoon, shortly after I started attending school for full days, Bobby, who only went in the mornings, thought he would do me a favor and change the water in the little bowl where I kept my pet green turtles Sarge and George. They'd come from the local five-and-ten.

I arrived home that afternoon and went directly to feed my turtles. But Sarge and George weren't hungry. They would never be hungry again. Bobby had unknowingly filled the bowl with boiling hot tap water. My turtles could not even escape to the little island with the plastic palm tree, for he had submerged it. I was angry at what he'd done and also frightened that he could have made such a dreadful mistake.

Just then Bobby and Mom walked into my room. "You stupid—" I started to shout and caught myself. Too late. Bobby's pale blue eyes, which according to my mother had not changed color since the day he was born, bloomed with hurt. Mom sent him out back to play. I felt horrible. I think she was as close to striking me as she would ever come. She grabbed my shoulders instead and said in a voice so full of seriousness and conviction it startled me, "Just remember, God put us here to help him."

Today Mom, who struggles with Alzheimer's, is in many ways more helpless than her retarded little boy was, and I'm ashamed to admit that I sometimes become impatient with her too. The other day, for instance, she refused to put on socks, all the while complaining noisily about how cold the floor felt on her bare feet. "Mom...," I sighed, exasperated. Part of it, I'm sure, is my sheer human irritability, and part of it, on a deeper level, is my fear that my mother is no longer someone I can reach to for help as I had for so many years.

But holding the pair of socks in my hand, I recalled something she taught me one day when I was little. I remember Bobby, who will be a little boy forever. And I remind myself: *We are here to help*.

Lord, I have received so much help in my life.
Help me to help others.

###

No Baths for Marty

O Lord, thou hast searched me, and known me.
Thou knowest my down-sitting and mine uprising,
thou understandest my thought afar off.
—Psalm 139:1–2

"Come here, Marty," I say with practiced nonchalance. Marty, my yellow Lab, is curled up under the coffee table in a tight ball, as if to make himself as small as possible and therefore somehow less visible, if not altogether invisible. He wears a doomed expression and refuses to return my gaze. The question I can never answer is this: How does he know when I am going to give him a bath?

For some reason this dog—who will joyously propel himself into a freezing lake in the dead of winter and practically refuse to come out—profoundly dreads the prospect of a quick, lukewarm bath. Through the years, I have learned to disguise my nefarious intentions. I don't put the towels and shampoo out where he can see them. I don't start running the bath water. I don't say the word *bath*; I don't even spell it out to my wife Julee when she asks what I'm up to. I conduct all the necessary preparations in complete secrecy. And still, he always knows.

How, Lord?

For some reason, I've never gotten an answer to that prayer.

Today I get down on all fours, rub his head, look at him and say, "It's okay, Mar-Mar. I'll be fast."

His liquid brown eyes look straight back at me as if to say, "Let's get it over with." No, not "as if." That is what he means. A spine-tingling sense of awe comes over me. I absolutely understand what this animal is thinking!

And then Marty is up, moving slowly like a prisoner going to the gallows. By the time I get to the bathroom, he is sitting in the tub, waiting.

Lord, maybe some day You will tell me how Marty knows he's getting a bath. In the meantime, thank You for the relationships we have with our animals... and for the miracle of communication.

TUNA SANDWICH
PEACE OFFERING

For he is our peace, who hath made both one, and hath broken
down the middle wall of partition between us.
—EPHESIANS 2:14

After more than twenty years of marriage, Julee and I are pretty good friends. We hardly ever fight anymore. But the other night we had one of our rare blowups.

I won't go into the details because it was over something predictably silly. At the time, though, we were serious. I went into my usual post-fight mode, retreating into a book, chancing an occasional aggrieved glare in my wife's direction while trying not to stoke the flames of the argument again. For her part, Julee clicked through the TV channels distractedly—coldly, I thought. I glanced at the clock. Is it time to walk the dogs yet? Could I just get out of here for a few minutes?

I was determined to let Julee make the first peace gesture. After all, she had started it. I hadn't helped, fighting right back when she lost her cool. But she shouldn't have pushed me. I'd had a lousy day, too, and I wasn't going to apologize. At least not before she did.

In the beginning of our marriage, this sort of nasty stalemate could go on for days. Back then, we didn't know how to fight. We had to learn how to have a disagreement, and accept that not every day of our lives together was going to be fair weather. Once, during one of these early matrimonial Armageddons, when Julee and I hadn't relaxed around each other for a couple of days, I impulsively ran home at lunch one noon with an inspired peace offering—tuna salad on a sesame bagel from her favorite neighborhood deli. What a miracle that simple sandwich worked!

Now I closed my book. "Tuna sandwich?" I asked. There are a lot of different ways to say you're sorry after twenty years.

Father, You have guided me through my marriage
much as a parent guides a child.
Our love alone is not enough; we need Yours.

###

STRETCH YOUR
MIND AND SOUL

I meditate on all that thou hast done....
I stretch out my hands to thee.
—PSALM 143:5–6 RSV

Every morning my wonderful dogs help remind me of a lesson in prayer I recently learned.

More or less at the crack of dawn, I crawl out of bed to leash up Sally, my peppy cocker spaniel, and Marty, my big yellow Lab, for their walk. But first they indulge in a morning ritual: stretching. Marty starts by doing his forelegs, then stretching out his hips and back legs, taking his time, carefully preparing his body for the rigors of his walk. While I get on my coat, Sally likes to jump up and use me to stretch against. After their walk, I rush over to the gym for a quick, heart-pounding workout. On the way I squeeze in some prayer.

This all came to an irritating halt recently when I

sustained a painful case of tendonitis in my lower right leg. "You've got to do your stretching," the trainer admonished me. I hate to stretch. It might be fine for dogs, but I am impatient with it. "Stretching before you work out prepares the muscles. It opens them up so they can grow," he explained.

For the next week I stopped at the gym only to soak my leg in the whirlpool. I was chagrined to find myself still squeezing in my morning prayer, rushing through it like just another chore to cross off. A friend to whom I mentioned this situation remarked, "Isn't meditation before prayer a little like stretching before exercise? You need to put yourself in God's presence before you can talk to Him." My friend—and the trainer—were onto something. *Stretching helps open up your muscles, so they can grow.*

That is why when I watch Sally and Marty stretch out now before their morning walk, I remind myself: *Take your time. Stretch your mind and soul for God before you pray. Open up and prepare to grow!*

God, work with me to stretch my prayer muscles.

A Note from the Publisher

Summerside Press is a division of Guideposts, a nonprofit organization that touches millions of lives every day through products and services that inspire, encourage, and uplift. Our books present a faith-based, uplifting view of the journey of life. Our mission is to help people connect their faith-filled values with their daily lives. To learn more, visit www.summersidepress.com